GAYM
COUNTY
GUIDES

West Sussex

First published by
Gaymer's Guides Limited,
24 Notting Hill Gate, London W11 3BR
Tel: 071-229 9944 Fax: 071-727 5442

Copyright © Gaymer's Guides Ltd. 1990
Gaymer's County Guides to West Sussex
ISBN 1-872173-02-0

British Library Cataloguing in Publication Data
Gaymer, Stephen Benjamin 1952-
West Sussex.
1. West Sussex - Visitors' guides
I. Title
914.22604858
ISBN 1-872173-02-0

Editor: Stephen Gaymer
Assistant Editor: Alison Ritchie
Original Design: Angel Bacon

Cover photograph
Arundel Castle

Printed by Whitstable Litho Printers Ltd., Whitstable, Kent.
Typeset in Palatino by Area Graphics, Letchworth.

The publishers would like to thank the
following for their assistance in the compilation of this guide:
Edward Crawshaw, Sebastian Grimes, English Heritage,
Andrew Lucas, John Stimpson,The National Trust.
Gaymer's Girls: Rose Bellingham, Sue Bushnell,
Sarah Chamberlain, Cythare Cooper,
Vicki-Jane Fuller, Lucy Gaymer.

CONTENTS

KEY TO ABBREVIATIONS

AA.	AUTOMOBILE ASSOCIATION	DOGS.	DOGS ALLOWED	RAC.	ROYAL AUTOMOBILE CLUB
AC.	ACCESS	ER.	EGON RONAY	V.	VISA
AM.	AMERICAN EXPRESS	F.	FUNCTIONS	VEG.	VEGETARIAN FOOD
B.	BANQUETS	M.	MICHELIN GUIDE		AVAILABLE
CF.	CONFERENCE FACILITIES	N/S.	NO SMOKING AREAS	W.	WEDDINGS
D.	DINERS CLUB	P.	PARTIES	W/CHAIR.	WHEELCHAIR ACCESS

POYNINGS FROM THE DOWNS

GAYMER'S COUNTY GUIDES are the first fully-illustrated comprehensive guide books that contain a gazetteer of every town, village and hamlet within a given area; they also list every hotel, guest house, restaurant and pub within that area, plus places of interest and churches. Other amenities are also included, such as art galleries, leisure and garden centres, cinemas and theatres, and so on. In short, Gaymer's County Guides list everything that may be of interest to visitors.

BALCOMBE VIADUCT

There are many publications which list some of these facilities, but none that list them all; they also tend to be selective. Gaymer's County Guides list everything, without qualification. However, by giving more details of certain establishments, it is left to the readers' discretion to decide whether a particular place suits their requirements.

At the back of the book are detailed indexes; the towns, the places of interest and illustrations are indexed alphabetically. Other amenities are cross-referenced, so that should a specific amenity be sought, for example a swimming-pool, it can be located.

The majority of establishments whose full details appear have paid a fee, and will have copies of this guide for sale. Although every effort has been made to include every establishment, there will inevitably be places that have been overlooked. We invite readers to send in details of omissions or inaccuracies.

Our aim is to produce a fully comprehensive and accurate representation of every relevant amenity in the county, that will serve as an invaluable aid to tourists and inhabitants alike.

CHICHESTER CATHEDRAL

LONG BEFORE THERE were any counties, man has inhabited the south-east of England, arriving by sea from France and the continent, and introducing skills and customs into the local culture. He has built camps, castles, villas, places of worship and palaces, some of which remain today. The Iron Age hill-forts at **Goodwood** and **Findon**, the Roman villa at **Bignor**, the Roman Palace at **Fishbourne**, the traces of ancient capitals on the **Selsey** peninsular, the medieval castles of **Arundel, Amberley** and **Bramber**, the cathedrals of **Chichester** and **Arundel**.

The word Sussex is derived from 'South Saxons', and was an entity before the Doomsday Book in 1086 documented the Kingdom, and it wasn't until 1889 that the large county of Sussex, with its 70 miles of coastline, was divided up into East and West by Royal Charter. In 1974 the boundaries were changed again by the Government, to even out the voting areas.

In Roman times, the capital of the county was at **Chichester**, revealed in the layout of its four main streets. The Roman Wall exists still in many places around the city. To the west is **Fishbourne**, once port to the Roman capital, and site of one of the most spectacular Roman palaces to be found anywhere. It stands at the tip of **Chichester Harbour**, once more navigable than today, and it was from the creek at **Bosham** that King Harold sailed to appease his cousin William, as recorded in the Bayeaux tapestry.

West Sussex can be divided neatly into three distinct sections; to the north, running east to west, the **Weald**; to the south the broad **coastal plain**, running parallel to the **English Channel**, and sandwiched between them, the famous **South Downs.**

It is impossible to describe modern West Sussex and its inhabitants without recognizing its proximity to London. The most northerly large town in Sussex, **Crawley**, is less than twenty miles from the centre of the metropolis, and many of those who live in the county commute every day into the city.

This has bestowed on **Sussex** an opulence that it would find difficult to support alone, and many of the carefully preserved farmhouses and cottages owe their continuing prosperity to salaries earned outside the county.

The **Weald**, in particular, reflects this phenomena. The word weald comes from the Anglo Saxon meaning 'wood', as all this part of the country was once one vast forest until it was cleared for agricultural purposes, and to fuel the iron workers' furnaces. Nowadays it is a curiously timeless landscape, with winding, undulating lanes between the scattered settlements. From almost everywhere in the **Weald** the South Downs can be seen on the southern horizon.

Once a major thoroughfare for prehistoric man, the **South Downs Way** follows the line of the hills from Hampshire all the way to **Eastbourne**, and the path is still well-trodden by modern day walkers. Never more than a couple of miles wide, the downs have for centuries played an important part in the region's history. There are views all around from the top of the downs, and Neolithic man built hill forts there, remains of which can still be seen at **Goodwood, Cissbury** and **Ditchling.**

Nearly every coastal village has connections, real or perceived, with smuggling, and it is obvious that much of it went on. From **Fishbourne** to **Rye**, many an illicit substance has been secretly rowed ashore to hidden coves at night. Although it usually thought that this contraband consisted of whisky and brandy, in fact at the time when it was heavily taxed, wool was the illicit substance.

Sussex-by-the-Sea has long invoked visions of holidays, and the coast is now almost completely devoted to the pursuit of leisure. There are the well-known holiday resorts of the **Witterings, Bognor Regis, Littlehampton** and **Worthing**, and the sailing centre at **Chichester Harbour**. Now the harbour is home to thousands of pleasure craft, who anchor in or near modern marinas. Chichester Harbour is one of the premier sailing areas in the country.

THE 15TH CENTURY MARKET CROSS, CHICHESTER

AMBERLEY MOUNT AND THE SOUTH DOWNS FROM BURY HILL

ADVERSANE

A village set around a T-Junction between Pulborough and Billingshurst.

HOTEL
Newstead Hotel
Tel: (0403) 783196

RESTAURANT
The Old House Restaurant
Stane Street. Tel: (040 381) 2186

PUBLIC HOUSE
The Blacksmiths Arms
Stane Street. Tel: (040 381) 2493

🐦 🐦 🐦 🐦 🐦 🐦 🐦

ALBOURNE

A Wealden village just off the main A23 road north of Brighton, with some fine Elizabethan houses. St Bartholomew's church, restored by the Victorians, has some Norman features.
Population: 533.

RESTAURANT
Shaved Thatch Restaurant
Tel: (079 156) 324

PUBLIC HOUSE
Kings Cafe Bar
London Road. Tel: (0273) 833143

OTHER AMENITY
GARDEN CENTRE
Hazelden Wholesale Nurseries
London Road. Tel: (0273) 832477

🐦 🐦 🐦 🐦 🐦 🐦 🐦

ALDINGBOURNE

One of the oldest and largest parishes in England dating from the 7th century, Aldingbourne is situated east of Chichester on the coastal plain between the English Channel and the South Downs. The wartime airfield of Tangmere is very close, but planes fly no longer, leaving the inhabitants in peace. There are some old flint cottages and barns at Norton, half a mile to the north.

7

Population: 2,690.

OTHER AMENITIES

CARAVAN PARK
Weir Associates
Beechfield Park , Hook Lane. Tel: (0903) 882226

GARDEN CENTRE
Limmer Pond Nurseries
Nyton Road. Tel: (0243) 543239

🐌 🐌 🐌 🐌 🐌 🐌 🐌

ALDWICK
One of the more pleasant suburbs of Bognor Regis. The Marine Gardens near the sea are very civilized, with fish-pond, putting-green and exotic plants. The Aldwick Bay Estate, east towards Pagham, has large expensive houses, one of which belongs to the Earl of Spencer, father to Princess Diana.

RESTAURANT
Marine Park Restaurant
Marine Drive West. Tel: (0243) 823137

🐌 🐌 🐌 🐌 🐌 🐌 🐌

ALFOLD

RESTAURANT
Chez Jean
Dunsfold Road. Tel: (0403) 752357

🐌 🐌 🐌 🐌 🐌 🐌 🐌

AMBERLEY
This ancient settlement stands at the northern end of the Arun gap. The river has silted up considerably since Amberley Castle was built, leaving them some distance apart. The castle was built in the 1370s, when the French were foraging up and down the South Coast, and King Charles was reputed to have stayed there on his flight to the coast after defeat at the Battle of Worcester in 1651. The peaceful village is built in a quadrant shape, with a pleasing mixture of thatch and tile, half-timbered, flint and brick houses, many with wisteria growing up their walls. There is a lively traditional village pub in the centre of the village. *Population: 516.*

PLACES OF INTEREST
Amberley Chalk Pits Museum

Tel: (0798) 831370
Museum making use of the old lime quarries, with some interesting exhibits.

RESTAURANT
Quins Restaurant
Houghton Bridge. Tel: (0798) 811790

PUBLIC HOUSE
The Sportsman
Rackham Road. Tel: (0798) 831787
The Black Horse
High Street. Tel: (0798) 831700

OTHER AMENITY
CARAVAN PARK
Houghton Bridge Tea Rooms & Caravan Park
BN18 9LP Tel: (0798) 831558
Months Open: April to October. Days Open: Monday to Sunday. Bank Holidays: BH open. Proprietors: Mr & Mrs B Mead.

🐌 🐌 🐌 🐌 🐌 🐌 🐌

ANGMERING
A pretty little village north-east of Littlehampton, situated around the village green and between two hills. The Victorian church has an interesting font, carved with flowers and leaves. *Population: 5,333.*

HOTEL
The Woodman Arms
Tel: (090 674) 240

GUEST HOUSE
Cherrymead Guest House
Station Road. Tel: (0903) 782119

RESTAURANT
La Casita Restaurant
Arundel Road. Tel: (0903) 775937

PUBLIC HOUSES
The Lamb Inn
The Square . Tel: (0903) 784499
The Spotted Cow
High Street. Tel: (0903) 783919

OTHER AMENITIES
GARDEN CENTRES

Manor Nurseries
High Street. Tel: (0903) 786977
Roundstone Garden Centre

Roundstone By Pass. Tel: (0903) 776481
Stonehurst
Dappers Lane . Tel: (0903) 784190
St. Denys Nursery
Dappers Lane. Tel: (0903) 773240

🐾 🐾 🐾 🐾 🐾 🐾 🐾

ANSTY

A pretty little village on a crossroads west of Haywards Heath.

PUBLIC HOUSE

Ansty Cross Inn
Cuckfield Road. Tel: (0444) 413038

🐾 🐾 🐾 🐾 🐾 🐾 🐾

APULDRAM

A village on Chichester Harbour which takes its name from the Old English word, 'apulder' or apple tree. This is orchard country. St Mary's church stands alone now, but in the 17th century was close to the original port for Chichester, of which nothing now remains.
Population: 167.

HOTEL

Crouchers Bottom Country Hotel
Birdham Road. Tel: (0243) 784995

🐾 🐾 🐾 🐾 🐾 🐾 🐾

ARDINGLY

A pleasant village, some three miles north of Haywards Heath, most noteworthy for hosting the annual South of England Agricultural show over three days in June. The permanent showground hosts a variety of events including regular and well attended antique fairs. The church of St Peter, dating from at least 770, has brasses showing Nicholas and Elizabeth Culpepper standing shoulder to shoulder with their ten sons and eight daughters!
Population: 1,580.

PLACES OF INTEREST

Wakehurst Place Garden
Tel: (0444) 892701
An extremely rich collection of exotic trees and shrubs amidst spectacular woodland valleys, streams and lakes. A garden for all seasons containing walled gardens, winter garden, water garden, heath gardens and Himalayan glade.
Months Open: All year. Days Open: Every day except New

ARUNDEL'S CATHOLIC CATHEDRAL

Year's Day and Christmas Day. Hours Open: 10am-7pm (summer) 10am-4pm (winter). Bank Holidays: Mostly open. Admission: £1.50. Children 60p.

RESTAURANT

The Oak Inn
Street Lane. Tel: (0444) 892244

🐾 🐾 🐾 🐾 🐾 🐾 🐾

ARUNDEL

From a distance Arundel has one of the most attractive vistas of any town, anywhere. (See front cover). The castle competes with the Catholic Cathedral and the South Downs to dominate the skyline, and the houses are clustered below. The pretty High Street sweeps down the hill from the castle to the bridge over the Arun, and is lined by hotels, pubs, restaurants, tea-shops and antique shops. The two other principle streets, Tarrant Street and Maltravers Street run at right angles to the High Street, and they too have their quota of tea-shops and antique shops. Indeed, there can be few towns in England which have more antique shops per head of population. They do, however, along with the castle, attract many visitors to this picturesque little town. The original castle was built on the River Arun to guard the 'Arun Gap' through the downs, immediately after the Norman Conquest, and the town grew around it. The present castle was built as recently as the turn of the century, in mock-medieval style; only the Keep is authentically Norman. Arundel is the country seat of the Duke of Norfolk, the Premier Duke and leading Catholic, hence the Catholic Cathedral. The previous duke's love of horse-racing is reflected in the town, with stables, jockeys and race horses abounding, whilst his widow, the Dowager Duchess Lavinia, annually hosts the opening match of international cricket touring sides. A grand avenue west of the castle leads to Swanbourne

9

ARUNDEL CASTLE BUILT ORIGINALLY TO GUARD THE ARUN GAP

Lake, a popular boating and recreational area, and to the Wildlife Park, the habitat of over a thousand wild birds.

Population: 2,162.

PLACES OF INTEREST

Arundel Castle
Tel: (0903) 882173

Arundel Toy & Military Museum
Tel: (0903) 882908

Famous teddy bears, dolls' houses, toy soldiers galore, "goss" china military models, dolls, tin toys, royal commemoratives, curiosities and small militaria.

Months Open: Easter to October. Days Open: Most days Easter to October, Weekends during winter and half term. Hours Open: 10.30-5.30pm (closed 1pm-2pm for lunch). Bank Holidays: Open all bank and school holidays. Admission: £1.25. Children £1.00. Car park and cafés nearby.

HOTELS

Arundel Resort Hotel
18 Chichester Road. Tel: (0903) 882677

Dukes of Arundel
65, High Street. Tel: (0903) 883847

Garrick Hotel
43, Tarrant Street. Tel: (0903) 883916

The Golden Goose Hotel
Station Road. Tel: (0903) 882588

Howards Hotel
Crossbush. Tel: (0903) 882655

Norfolk Arms Hotel & Restaurant
High Street. Tel: (0903) 882101

St. Mary's Gate Inn
London Road. Tel: (0903) 883145

A small country hotel offering high standards of cuisine and comfortable bedrooms, all en-suite, telephones, colour TV's etc.

BEDROOMS: B&B £ 32.50. 2 Double, (2 en suite, 2 TV, 2 phone, 2 tea/coffee) B&B £ 50.00. 6 Twin, (6 en suite, 6 TV, 6 phone, 6 tea/coffee) B&B £ 50.00. 2 Family, (2 en suite, 2 TV, 2 phone, 2 tea/coffee) £ 65.00. RESTAURANT: Lunch: £ 8.50. Dinner: £ 10.50. House Wine: £ 6.25. Specialities: Gourmet dinners Saturday evenings. Credit Cards: Ac. Am. D. V.

Weekend Breaks: 2 nights: £ 99.00.

The Swan Hotel
High Street. Tel: (0903) 882314

The White Hart
Tel: (0903) 882374

GUEST HOUSES

Arden Guest House
4 Queens Lane. Tel: (0903) 882544

Arundel House Guest House
11 High Street. Tel: (0903) 882136

Bridge House
18 Queen Street. Tel: (0903) 882779

RESTAURANTS

Arun Tandoori Restaurant
Tarrant Street. Tel: (0903) 884204

Belinda's Restaurant
13, Tarrant Street. Tel: (0903) 882977

Cafe des Amis
Crossbush. Tel: (0903) 882655

The Castle View Hotel
63, High Street. Tel: (0903) 883029

The Copper Kettle
21, Tarrant Street. Tel: (0903) 883679

The Crown House Restaurant
41a, High Street. Tel: (0903) 882025

Hemingways Diner
33, High Street. Tel: (0903) 883378

Pogey's
25, Tarrant Street. Tel: (0903) 882222

Violette Cafe
67, High Street. Tel: (0903) 883702

PUBLIC HOUSES

The Eagle
41 Tarrant Street. Tel: (0903) 882304

The General Abercrombie
4 / 6 Queen Street. Tel: (0903) 882347

Kings Arms
36 Tarrant Street. Tel: (0903) 882312

Plough & Sail Inn
Crossbush. Tel: (0903) 883118

The Red Lion
45 High Street. Tel: (0903) 882597

The White Hart
3 Queen Street. Tel: (0903) 882374

CAFES & TEA ROOMS

Country Kitchen
31b Tarrant Street. Tel: (0903) 882438

Lower Lodge Cafe
Arundel Castle. Tel: (0903) 883836

The Tea Garden
Arundel Castle. Tel: (0903) 882171

OTHER AMENITIES

ART GALLERIES

The Armstrong-Davis Gallery
High Street. Tel: (0903) 882752

River Gallery
25 High Street. Tel: (0903) 882177

CARAVAN PARK

Maynards Caravan Park
Crossbush. Tel: (0903) 882075

FISH FARM

Chalk Springs Fishery
Park Bottom. Tel: (0903) 883742
Other site open to the public at 'The Castle Front Feeding Pond',
Mill Road, Arundel, West Sussex. Tel: 0903 883742.

GARDEN CENTRE

Arundel Arboretum
Scotland Barn , Chichester Road. Tel: (0903) 883251

TAXIS

Arundel Area Car Hire
Arundel Station Approach, The Causeway. Tel: (0903) 882418

Arundel Cab Co- Taxis
43 Tarrant Street. Tel: (0903) 882591

Garys Taxis
Crossbush Cottage, Crossbush. Tel: (0903) 883831

THEATRE

The Priory Playhouse
London Road. Tel: (0903) 883345

❧ ❧ ❧ ❧ ❧ ❧ ❧

ASHINGTON

A 'bungalow' village, to the north of the downs between London and Worthing.
Population: 1,704.

PLACES OF INTEREST

Warren Hill
Tel: (0903) 892523

HOTEL

Mill House Hotel and Restaurant
Mill Lane. Tel: (0903) 892426

RESTAURANT

Ashington Court Restaurant
London Road. Tel: (0903) 892575

PUBLIC HOUSE

The Red Lion
London Road. Tel: (0903) 892226

OTHER AMENITIES

CAR HIRE

Aristocars
Virginia Cottage, London Road. Tel: (0903) 892410

FISH FARM

Ashington Trout Farm
New Trout Farm , Hoe Street. Tel: (0903) 893066

GARDEN CENTRES

Holy Gate Cactus Nursery
Billingshurst Lane. Tel: (0903) 892930
Peter Smith
Rectory Lane. Tel: (0903) 892870
Stanford Nurseries
Malthouse Farm , Malthouse Lane. Tel: (0903) 892337
Laurence Hobbs Orchids
Hollage Plant Centre , Billingshurst Lane. Tel: (0903) 893017

ASHURST

A remote Wealden village north of Steyning, near the River Adur. The 12th century St James' church has one of the prettiest exteriors in the county. There are some fine 16th century houses in the village.
Population: 262.

PUBLIC HOUSE

Fountain
B2135. Tel: (0403) 710219

BALCOMBE

A village half way between Crawley and Haywards Heath with some large historical houses from the 17th and 18th centuries. Nearby the London-Brighton railway line tunnels under the forest to the north, and to the south crosses the River Ouse via the spectacular Balcombe Viaduct, which boasts thirty seven arches.
Population: 1,634.

HOTELS

The Half Moon
Haywards Heath Road. Tel: (0444) 811373
Highley Manor
Crawley Lane. Tel: (0444) 811711

PUBLIC HOUSE

Cowdray Arms
London Road. Tel: (0444) 811280

BALLS CROSS

Attractive cottages, and a pub that, uniquely in England, doubles as a polling-station at election times.

PUBLIC HOUSE

The Stag Inn
Tel: (040 377) 241

BARNHAM

Barnham is best-known to generations of holiday-makers for its station; it is the junction for trains that take the spur lines to Bognor Regis and Littlehampton on the London Victoria-Portsmouth line. Situated on the coastal plain, in the Middle Ages Barnham stood on a tidal creek, and was a fishing village. Barnham is generally unprepossessing, but does have some nice old houses and an attractive part-Norman church, St. Mary.
Population: 619.

HOTEL

Barnham Hotel
28 Barnham Road. Tel: (0243) 552272

RESTAURANTS

Barnham Fish Bar
41 Barnham Road. Tel: (0243) 551021
The Lantern House
45 Barnham Road. Tel: (0243) 553881

PUBLIC HOUSE

Murrell Arms
Yapton Road. Tel: (0243) 553320

MEET AT THE

MURRELL ARMS
BARNHAM

• • •

SUSSEX
FRIARY & BURTON
On Tap

• • •

ENGLISH COUNTRY WINES

• • •

GOOD ORDINARY FOOD

Unchanged village pub decorated with coaching and drinking memorabilia. Large garden with vineyard. Music Thursdays and alternate Sundays. Antique auctions fortnightly.
Brewery: Friary Meux Ltd. Licensee: Mr Mervyn Cotton. Opening Hours: Mon-Fri 11.00-2.30, 6.00-11.00; Open all day Saturday; Sunday 12.00-2.00, 7-10.30. Beer available: Friary, Burton, King & Barnes Sussex. Food available: 12.00-2.00, 6.00-10.00. Garden. Car Park. Traditional games: Ring the bull, shove ha'penny, darts, cribbage.

OTHER AMENITIES
FLORISTS
Octagon Flowers
21 The Square. Tel: (0243) 552769

GARDEN CENTRES
Croftway Nursery & Garden Centre
Yapton Road. Tel: (0243) 552121
J.P. McCorquodale
39 Hill Lane. Tel: (0243) 552344
Mapletrees Nursery
Yapton Road. PO22 0BQ Tel: (0243) 552028
Mayfields Nursery & Garden Centre
Yapton Road. Tel: (0243) 551235

🐑 🐑 🐑 🐑 🐑 🐑 🐑

BARNS GREEN
A small hamlet between Billingshurst and Horsham.

PUBLIC HOUSE
The Queens Head
Chapel Road. Tel: (0403) 730436

OTHER AMENITY
CAR HIRE
E.& B. Knight
Batchelor Cottage, Emms Lane. Tel: (0403) 730438

🐑 🐑 🐑 🐑 🐑 🐑 🐑

BAYNARDS

PUBLIC HOUSE
The Thurlow Arms
Tel: (040 372) 2459

🐑 🐑 🐑 🐑 🐑 🐑 🐑

BEEDING

HOTEL

The Kings Head Inn
High Street. Tel: (0903) 812196

PUBLIC HOUSE
The Rising Sun
Shoreham Road. Tel: (0903) 814424

OTHER AMENITY
CARAVAN PARK
Country Side Farm
Church Lane. Tel: (0903) 814360

🐑 🐑 🐑 🐑 🐑 🐑 🐑

BEPTON
A sandstone and half-timber village beneath the downs, south-west of Midhurst. The original settlement of farm and church sit on a mound, with fine views south of Bepton Down.
Population: 95.

HOTEL
Park House Hotel
Tel: (073 081) 2880

PUBLIC HOUSE
The Country Inn
Severals Road. Tel: (073 081) 3466

🐑 🐑 🐑 🐑 🐑 🐑 🐑

BIGNOR
A small village in the lee of the downs consisting of a quadrant of lanes surrounding the church. At the east end of the village is 'the Old Shop', an unrestored 15th century yeoman's half-timbered and thatched cottage, one of the most photographed buildings in the county. To the west of the village lie the remains of one of the largest Roman villas in the country, just off Stane Street. On nearby Bignor Hill is the site of a Neolithic causewayed camp.
Population: 105.

PLACES OF INTEREST
Roman Villa
Tel: (079 87) 259

🐑 🐑 🐑 🐑 🐑 🐑 🐑

BILLINGSHURST
A bustling old coaching town on Stane Street, set in a small valley between two hills. Billingshurst has been linked with Billingsgate, which is where Stane Street enters the City of London. Inns and shops

13

line the main street.

Population: 5,301.

GUEST HOUSES

Basset Fee House
2 High Street. Tel: (040 381) 2806
Stanmore Guest House
118 High Street. Tel: (040 381) 2922

RESTAURANTS

Badgers Restaurant
87, High Street. Tel: (040 381) 3547
Crosby's Restaurant
92, High Street. Tel: (040 381) 2432
Il Cappuccino Restaurant Pizzeria
9, Jengers Mead. Tel: (040 381) 2910
Lannards Restaurant
Okehurst Road. Tel: (040 381) 4626
The New Town Chinese Restaurant
5, Jengers Mead. Tel: (040 381) 3484
Tandoori Village Restaurant
42, High Street. Tel: (040 381) 4735/4890

PUBLIC HOUSES

Kings Arms
80 High Street. Tel: (040 381) 2072
The Kings Head
40 High Street. Tel: (040 381) 2921
Limeburners Arms
Newbridge. Tel: (040 381) 2311
Railway Inn
Station Road. Tel: (040 378) 2928
Comfortable house by railway station. Real ale specialists.
Top value food.
Brewery: Whitbread. Licensee: Mr Ian King. Opening Hours: 11.00-3.00, 5.30-11.00. Beer available: Flowers OB, Marstons Pedigree, Strongs Country, Pompey Royal, Heineken, Stella, Bitter, Mild, Murphys, Guinness, draught cider. Food available: all day. 3 Bedrooms: B&B per person: £ 13.00. Car park. Traditional games: Darts, bar billiards.
Ye Olde Six Bells
76 High Street. Tel: (040 381) 2124

CAFES & TEA ROOMS

Burdock Tea Shop
59 High Street. Tel: (040 381) 2750
Sallys Cafe
9a Lower Station Road . Tel: (040 381) 2017

OTHER AMENITIES

ART GALLERY
Lannard Gallery
Okehurst Lane. Tel: (040 381) 2692

HEALTH CLUB
Coconut
Woodyards Cottage , Daux Road. Tel: (040 381) 2064

TAXI
Billingshurst Taxi Service
Wilkins House, 36 Station Road. Tel: (0403) 783652/784578

🐾 🐾 🐾 🐾 🐾 🐾 🐾

BINSTED

A tiny hamlet best known latterly for its excellent pub. The road peters out into a farm track, a cul-de-sac of country calm in this well populated part of Sussex.

PUBLIC HOUSE

The Black Horse
Binsted Lane. Tel: (0243) 551213

🐾 🐾 🐾 🐾 🐾 🐾 🐾

BIRDHAM

The 'Birdham Strait' is well known to budding Formula One racing drivers testing how fast their cars can go. Unfortunately, some go too fast, and consequently the 'strait' is a notorious accident black-spot. Birdham itself is squeezed between the road and one of the many shores of Chichester Harbour. There is a big marina here, and Birdham pool, so the area is very popular with yachtsmen. This is an affluent area, and there are many expensive houses. The yachts in the harbour make an invigorating site.
Population: 1,412.

RESTAURANT

The Birdham Tea Parlour
Main Road. Tel: (0243) 511341

PUBLIC HOUSE

The Bell Inn
Bell Lane. Tel: (0243) 512279

OTHER AMENITIES

CARAVAN PARK
Bell Caravan Park
Bell Lane. PO20 7HY Tel: (0243) 512264

GARDEN CENTRES
Earnley Gardens
133 Almodington Lane. Tel: (0243) 512637
Koolbergen & Ramsey

ONE OF THE MOST PHOTOGRAPHED BUILDINGS IN THE COUNTY, THE OLD SHOP, BIGNOR (PAGE 13)

Selden Bell Lane. Tel: (0243) 512184
Russell's Garden Centre
Main Road. PO20 7BY Tel: (0243) 512525

MARINA
Chichester Yacht Basin
Tel: (0243) 512731

🍎 🍎 🍎 🍎 🍎 🍎 🍎

BOGNOR REGIS

Bognor was in the centre of three or four other, older, settlements, that cemented the whole resort together when it was created in the early 19th century, largely by one man, Sir Richard Hotham. Bognor has a loyal and faithful clientele who return every year to enjoy its long promenade, its golden sands and record amounts of sunshine. George V convalesced here, in the now demolished Craigwell House, and on his recovery awarded the town with its 'Regis'. Upon his further demise, and in response to the suggestion that he return to the town for more recuperation,

he was reputed to have uttered the now immortal words 'Bugger Bognor'. Butlin's Holiday Camp, to the east of the town, is now renamed South Coast World.

HOTELS
Alancourt Hotel
Marine Drive West. Tel: (0243) 864844
The Ancient Mariner Hotel
West Street. Tel: (0243) 821797
Argyle Private Hotel
Norfolk Square. Tel: (0243) 865647
Belle Vue Hotel
Waterloo Square. Tel: (0243) 863434/863463
Black Mill House Hotel
25 Princess Avenue. Tel: (0243) 821945/865596
Carlton Hotel
Esplanade. Tel: (0243) 823656
Gables Hotel
28 Crescent Road. Tel: (0243) 865830
Hilary Hotel
Park Road. Tel: (0243) 821259
Homestead Private Hotel

90 Aldwick Road. Tel: (0243) 823443
Pixie Hotel & Restaurant
Waterloo Square. Tel: (0243) 823692
The Royal Hotel
Esplanade. Tel: (0243) 864665
The Royal Norfolk Hotel
The Esplanade. Tel: (0243) 826222
Russell Hotel
Kings Parade. Tel: (0243) 823572
Seacrest Private Hotel
19 Nyewood Lane South. Tel: (0243) 821438
Selwood Lodge Hotel
93 Victoria Drive. Tel: (0243) 865071
Steyne Cottage Hotel
1 The Steyne. Tel: (0243) 865972
Steyne House
10 West Street. Tel: (0243) 828476
Victoria Hotel
32 Aldwick Road. Tel: (0243) 822335

GUEST HOUSES

Denleigh Guest House
28 Nyewood Lane. Tel: (0243) 866358
Jubilee Guest House
5 Gloucester Road. Tel: (0243) 863016
Mimosa Guest House
Alexandra Terrace, Clarence Road. Tel: (0243) 865588
Regis Lodge
3 Gloucester Road. Tel: (0243) 827110

RESTAURANTS

Beach Restaurant
Waterloo Square. Tel: (0243) 863437
Bellapais Restaurant
73 High Street. Tel: (0243) 863933
The Bersted Fish Bar
9 Royal Parade. Tel: (0243) 865080
Bombay Tandoori Restaurant
31a Station Road. Tel: (0243) 864038/826324
Carousel Licenced Restaurant
21 Lennox Street. Tel: (0243) 863409
Chips
61 Aldwick Road. Tel: (0243) 825177
Chuffers
4 Station Road. Tel: (0243) 820259
Cosy Fishbar
231 Chichester Road. Tel: (0243) 822893
Crumbs
9 The Arcade. Tel: (0243) 828151
Fai's Kitchen
64 Aldwick Road. Tel: (0243) 863427
Family Inn
Waterloo Square. Tel: (0243) 866464
The Fish Inn

Unit 4, Lennox Street. Tel: (0243) 825000
The Forsyth Saga
31 West Street. Tel: (0243) 862404
Golden Fish Bar
1 Duriston Parade, Duriston Drive. Tel: (0243) 862512
The Happy Friar
17 The Precinct, West Meads. Tel: (0243) 864931
Highfield Fish Bar
96 Highfield Road. Tel: (0243) 863089
Jasmine House Chinese Restaurant
23 Station Road. Tel: (0243) 863563
Katrinas Sandwich Bar
7 Lennox Street. Tel: (0243) 862533
Kay's
1 Albert Chambers, Sudley Road. Tel: (0243) 862533
The Kebab Machine
Waterloo Square. Tel: (0243) 830748
Kentucky Fried Chicken
4 Central Building, London Road. Tel: (0243) 863038
Kingsway Restaurant
12 The Queensway. Tel: (0243) 868837
Lacey's Bistro
5 Argyle Circus. Tel: (0243) 867489
The Lantern House
14 The Precinct. Tel: (0243) 821537
A Good Eating Guide featured restaurant. For Chinese food with a difference. Take away service available.
Chinese Cuisine. Specialities: Koong Po dishes, Aromatic Duck, Steamed Fish, Grilled Prawn, All Cantonese Style. Hours Open: Lunch: 12.00-2.00. Dinner: 5.00-11.30. Lunch: £ 3.45. House Wine: £ 5.50. Credit Cards: Ac. Am. D. V. Seating Capacity: 40. W/Chair.
Linden Fisheries
1 Linden Road. Tel: (0243) 865610
The Lotus House
52 Chichester Road. Tel: (0243) 863537
Magna Restaurant
33 Argyle Road. Tel: (0243) 863639
Manhattan
51a High Street. Tel: (0243) 863347
Manners Restaurant
1 Manor Place. Tel: (0243) 820512
Marine Fish Bar
23 West Street. Tel: (0243) 822106
McDonald's Hamburgers
41-43 High Street. Tel: (0243) 821459
Michael's
29 Queensway. Tel: (0243) 822387
Nelson's Restaurant
6 High Street. Tel: (0243) 860703
New Crystal
31 Station Road. Tel: (0243) 86523
The New Orleans
80 Little High Street, Waterloo Square. Tel: (0243) 863761

Ocean Fish Bar
23 Hawthorn Road. Tel: (0243) 827913
Paradise Med
2 The Steyne. Tel: (0243) 865106
The Pasta Place
49 Aldwick Road. Tel: (0243) 865555
Pickwick's Oven
16 Station Road. Tel: (0243) 866251
Poppins Restaurant
14 Queensway. Tel: (0243) 863765
Provencal Restaurant
31 Nyewood Lane. Tel: (0243) 822334
Rapley's
6-7 Lansdowne House, The Esplanade. Tel: (0243) 823958
Shahenshah Take Away
43 Queensway. Tel: (0243) 865033
Shelley's Restaurant
Marine Drive West. Tel: (0243) 865208
Speedy Pizzas
25 Station Road. Tel: (0243) 862000/830430
The Summerhouse
10 York Road. Tel: (0243) 825482
Sunrise
12 Royal Parade, Central Avenue. Tel: (0243) 863652
Wimpy Restaurant
17 The Arcade. Tel: (0243) 865226

PUBLIC HOUSES

The Alex
London Road. Tel: (0243) 863308
Licensee: Mr TJ Williams.
Berkeley Arms
West Street. Tel: (0243) 826878
Bilko's Club
14 Park Road. Tel: (0243) 825820
The Claremont
Scott Street. Tel: (0243) 865482
The Crown
Manor Place. Tel: (0243) 865645
Elizabeth II
3 The Steyne. Tel: (0243) 865751
Friary Arms
Shripney Road. Tel: (0243) 823373
Laburnum Public House
Laburnum Grove. Tel: (0243) 829411
The Lamb Inn
36 Steyne Street. Tel: (0243) 868215
The Martlets
Aldwick Road. Tel: (0243) 863560
The Orlando
High Street. Tel: (0243) 863883
Prince of Wales
Upper Bognor Road. Tel: (0243) 829633
The Railway Hotel
49 London Road. Tel: (0243) 865893
The Richmond Arms
224 London Road. Tel: (0243) 865460
The Ship Inn
Aldwick Street. Tel: (0243) 865334
Stamps
351 Chichester Road. Tel: (0243) 823744
Terminus Hotel
26 Station Road. Tel: (0243) 865674
The Unicorn
High Street. Tel: (0243) 865536
Having been an hotel since 1870, the Unicorn features strongly on tradition, which is reflected in its olde worlde image.
Brewery: Horndean Inns (subsidiary of Gales Ales). Licensee: Mr & Mrs Jim Torrent. OPEN ALL DAY. Opening Hours: 11.00-11.00 in the season. Beer available: HSB, BBB, Gales Best Bitter, dark mild, LA beer, Lager, cider. Food available: 12.00-5.00, 7.00-9.00. 6 Bedrooms: B&B per person: £ 15.00. Traditional games: Shove ha'penny, cribbage, dominoes, cards, dice games.
Victoria Inn
Charlwood Street. Tel: (0243) 864811
Waterloo Inn
Waterloo Square. Tel: (0243) 824231
The Wheatsheaf
85 Hawthorn Road. Tel: (0243) 864193
The White Horse
39 Chichester Road. Tel: (0243) 823994

CAFES & TEA ROOMS

Celebrity Cafe
33 Station Road. Tel: (0243) 863696
The Coffee House
7 Clock Walk, High Street. Tel: (0243) 861522
Dutch Oven Cafe
7 West Street. Tel: (0243) 820625
Gypsys
1 West Street. Tel: (0243) 860688
The Lennox Cafe
19 Wanstead Chambers, Lennox Road. Tel: (0243) 864818
Macari's Esplanade Cafe
46a London Road. Tel: (0243) 863753
Rock Lobster Seafood Restaurant
5 Waterloo Square. Tel: (0243) 825914
Rosie Lee
160 London Road. Tel: (0243) 827066

OTHER AMENITIES

ART GALLERY
Gough Bros. Art Shop & Gallery
71 High Street. Tel: (0243) 823773

17

BUS & COACH SERVICES
Southdown Motor Services
4 York Road. Tel: (0243) 865024

CAR HIRE/CHAUFFEUR DRIVE
Bognor Regis Taxi Association
The Kiosk, Railway Station. Tel: (0243) 865564
Classic Limousines
Waltham House, Town Cross Avenue. Tel: (0243) 860191

CAR HIRE/SELF DRIVE
Bruce Dixon (1949) Ltd.
Spencer Street. PO21 1AN Tel: (0243) 865718/865719
Cheap Car Hire
2 The Parade, Argyle Road. PO21 1DT Tel: (0243) 862172
Ford Rent-a-Car [W. Jones & Sons Ltd]
Lennox Street. Tel: (0243) 864641
Regis Rentals
6a Brazwick Avenue. Tel: (0243) 867055
Regis Service Station
449 Chichester Road. Tel: (0243) 828231

CARAVAN PARKS
Old Canal Caravan Camp
Lidsey Road. Tel: (0243) 543168
Poplars Caravan Park
Shripney Road. Tel: (0243) 820515
Riverside Caravan Centre
Riverside Park, Shripney Road. Tel: (0243) 865823/4/5

CINEMA
Cannon Cinema
51 Canada Grove. Tel: (0243) 823138

FLORISTS
Global Flowers
8 High Street. Tel: (0243) 820207
Town Flowers
Bedford Street. Tel: (0243) 826359
Nichola Weller NDSF
117 Chichester Road. PO21 5AE Tel: (0243) 820065
West End Florists
53 Aldwick Road. Tel: (0243) 824917

GARDEN CENTRE
Chalcroft Nurseries & Garden Centre
Chalcroft Lane . Tel: (0243) 863346

HEALTH CLUB
Images
47 High Street. Tel: (0243) 861341

HOLIDAY CAMP
South Coast World
Upper Bognor Road. Tel: (0243) 820202

NIGHT CLUBS
Bentley's Nightclub
The Esplanade. Tel: (0243) 827688
Nightclub/Disco
Months Open: All year round. Days Open: Tuesday - Sunday. Hours Open: 9.30pm-2.00am. Bank Holidays: open. Manager: Mr Paul Robinson.
Sheiks Nightclub & Disco
The Pier, The Esplanade. Tel: (0243) 820654/863786
Toppers Night Club
Bradlaw House, 5 Sudley Road. Tel: (0243) 865834

SAUNAS
Dial-a-Tan
39 Glamis Street. Tel: (0243) 820187
Reelaks
Sussex Street. Tel: (0243) 829684

STORES
FJ Bobby of Bognor
1 London Road. Tel: (0243) 864224
Marks & Spencer plc
40 London Road. Tel: (0243) 825425
Reynolds & Co. (Furnishers)
27/31 High Street. Tel: (0243) 864745

TAXIS
Abcabs
Waltham House, Town Cross Avenue. Tel: (0243) 862424
Bee's Taxi Service
135 Collyer Avenue. Tel: (0243) 825023
Bognor Railway Station Taxi Rank
Station Yard. Tel: (0243) 865651
Bognor Town Taxis
91 Essex Road. Tel: (0243) 864424
Revis Taxis
4 Laburnum Grove. Tel: (0243) 826127
Yellow Star Cab Company
South Bersted Garage, Shripney Road. Tel: (0243) 820222

THEATRE
Bognor Regis Centre
Belmont Street. Tel: (0243) 865551/865915
Entertainments Centre
Months Open: All. Days Open: Monday to Sunday. Hours Open: 9am - 11pm. Bank Holidays: open. Huge variety of professional and semi-professional shows. Home of the birdman rally, international clowns convention, autumn amble.

ALEXANDRA THEATRE

Lighting: Eurolight Micron Board x 96 ways
Sound: A.H.B. 16 Way Desk. P.A. Power up to 2K
NB: No grid

ROYAL HALL

Lighting: Electrosonic Sonic Board x 20 ways
Sound: A.H.B. 24 Way Desk. P.A. Power up to 2K
Mobile staging
NB: No grid

BOGNOR **REGIS** CENTRE
BOX OFFICE (0243) 865551

WATER SPORTS
Surfhog
7 Aldwick Road. Tel: (0243) 867945

ZOO
Rainbows End Adventure Park
Hotham Park, High Street. Tel: (0243) 825255

🐾 🐾 🐾 🐾 🐾 🐾 🐾

BOLNEY

A village close to the International Show Jumping ground at Hickstead. Parts of the church are Norman. The proximity of the A23 has robbed this village of any tranquility.
Population: 1,045.

HOTEL

Hickstead Resort Hotel
Jobs Lane. Tel: (044 46) 48023

PUBLIC HOUSES

The Bolney Stage
London Road. Tel: (044 482) 312
Eight Bells
The Street. Tel: (044 482) 396
Queens Head Inn
London Road. Tel: (0444) 881322

OTHER AMENITY

FISH FARM
Bolney Farm Shop
The Nurseries , London Road. Tel: (044 482) 350

🐾 🐾 🐾 🐾 🐾 🐾 🐾

BOSHAM

Bosham is, without doubt, one of the most charming and picturesque villages on the whole of the South Coast, and with a history to match its looks. It is dramatically situated around one of the irregular inlets of Chichester Harbour, with the downs in the distance. Bosham, with Holy Trinity church in the background, viewed from across the harbour, has to be one of the most painted scenes in Sussex. The church itself is situated on an ancient site, and King Canute's daughter is buried here. She drowned in the mill stream, alongside the church, and perhaps because of this Canute connection, Bosham claims that it was here that he ordered back the waves. It will never be proven, but it is fact that King Harold sailed from here to Normandy on that ill-fated trip in 1064, to pacify his cousin William. The fact that he failed, and that the Nor-

man conquest happened as a direct result, gives Bosham a unique place in English history. A charming pub overlooks the water, and when the tide is out unsuspecting customers park their cars under its windows. It gives the locals much entertainment to see them gradually submerge as the tide comes in. What was once a fishing village has been overtaken by the weekend cottage syndrome, with the subsequent rise in house prices. Bosham has lost a lot of its identity as a result, but it looks very good on it.
Population: 3,760.

HOTELS

Berkeley Arms
Bosham Lane. Tel: (0243) 573167
The Millstream Hotel
Bosham Lane. Tel: (0243) 573234
This beautiful 18th Century country house hotel, situated in picturesque Bosham, offers attractive modernised bedrooms, comfortable lounge and excellent restaurant.
*BEDROOMS: 5 Single, (5 en suite, 5 TV, 5 phone, 5 tea/coffee) B&B £ 55.00 - £ 65.00. 15 Double, (15 en suite, 15 TV, 15 phone, 15 tea/coffee) B&B £ 85.00. 9 Twin, (9 en suite, 9 TV, 9 phone, 9 tea/coffee) B&B £ 85.00 - £ 90.00. RESTAURANT: European Cuisine. Lunch: £ 13.50. Tea: £ 2.50. Dinner: £ 17.00. House Wine: £ 8.75. À La Carte: £ 15.50. HOTEL INFORMATION: CF. W. B. F. 40 space Car Park. Dogs by arrangement. Credit Cards: Ac. Am. D. V. Recommendations: AA**. ER. M. RAC**. Weekend Breaks: 2 nights: £ 102.00. 3 nights: £ 153.00. Allowance towards dinner: £ 14.50.*

RESTAURANTS

Bosham Inn
Main Road. Tel: (0243) 575027
Southsea Chinese Take Away
Delling Lane. Tel: (0243) 572704
The Wishing Well Tandoori
Main Road. Tel: (0243) 572234/575016

PUBLIC HOUSES

The Anchor Bleu
High Street. Tel: (0243) 573956
The White Swan
Main Road. Tel: (0243) 573381

OTHER AMENITIES

ART GALLERY
The Cumberland Gallery
High Street. Tel: (0243) 573725

CAR HIRE/SELF DRIVE
Bosham Service Station
Bosham Lane. Tel: (0243) 572211

BOSHAM HARBOUR, ONE OF THE MOST PAINTED SCENES IN SUSSEX

GARDEN CENTRE
The French Gardens Nursery & Garden Centre
Ratham Lane. Tel: (0243) 573388

WATER SPORTS
Bosham Sailing
Bosham Lane, Old Bosham. PO18 8HP Tel: (0243) 572555

🐚 🐚 🐚 🐚 🐚 🐚 🐚

BOXGROVE
Built on the site of a 12th century priory, ruins of which remain, Boxgrove has an important church, but is a surprisingly small single-street village.
Population: 752.

🐚 🐚 🐚 🐚 🐚 🐚 🐚

BRACKLESHAM BAY
A modern collection of hotels, holiday camps, and associated holiday paraphernalia.

RESTAURANTS
Clifford Cottages Restaurant
Bracklesham Lane. Tel: (0243) 670250

Ye Olde Farmhouse Restaurant
Holdens Farm, Bracklesham Lane. Tel: (0243) 670570
Mike's Restaurant
Bracklesham Lane. Tel: (0243) 671212
Moby's Fish Bar
Bracklesham Lane. Tel: (0243) 670748
Number One
1 Azara Parade, Bracklesham Lane. Tel: (0243) 671336

PUBLIC HOUSE
The Lively Lady
Bracklesham Lane. Tel: (0243) 670541

CAFE/TEA ROOMS
The Merry Chef
3 Azara Parade, Bracklesham Lane. Tel: (0243) 670552

OTHER AMENITIES
CARAVAN PARK
Holdens Farm Caravan Park
Bracklesham Lane. Tel: (0243) 670207/670406

FLORISTS
A. & P. Clay
Wynal, Bracklesham Lane. Tel: (0243) 670247

TAXI
Bracklesham Taxis
22 Elm Close. Tel: (0243) 670463

🐦 🐦 🐦 🐦 🐦 🐦 🐦

BRAMBER

'Brymmburh', Saxon for 'fortified hill', was once a large port until the River Adur silted up. The large Norman castle, mostly dismantled in the Civil War, guarded the Adur Gap. Only some of the walls and the castle gateway remain. Bramber's most famous Member of Parliament was William Wilberforce, the anti-slavery campaigner, who was elected in the days before the Reform Bill when Bramber returned two members for less than one hundred inhabitants. Charles II was reputed to have stayed here en route to his escape to France from Shoreham in 1651.
Population: 716.

PLACES OF INTEREST
House of Pipes
Tel: (0903) 812122
St. Mary's (pictured below)
Tel: (0903) 816205

RESTAURANTS
Brambers Supper Rooms
5, High Street. Tel: (0903) 812408
The Maharaja Restaurant
Tel: (0903) 814746
The Old Tollgate Restaurant
Tel: (0903) 813362

PUBLIC HOUSE
The Castle Hotel
The Street. Tel: (0903) 812102

OTHER AMENITY
CARAVAN PARK
Downland Mobile Home Park
The Street. Tel: (0903) 815291

🐦 🐦 🐦 🐦 🐦 🐦 🐦

BROADBRIDGE HEATH

On the Guildford road to the north-west of Horsham, close to the upper reaches of the River Arun.

HOTEL
The Shelley Arms Hotel
Billingshurst Road. Tel: (0403) 53406

RESTAURANT
Happy Eater Family Restaurant
1, Guildford Road. Tel: (0403) 68566

OTHER AMENITIES
CAR HIRE
Vauxhall Rental
Billingshurst Road. Tel: (0403) 56464
Unlimited mileage. AA, RAC cover. Special weekend and holiday rates.

GARDEN CENTRE
Newbridge Nurseries
The Bungalow, Billingshurst Road. Tel: (0403) 65731

LEISURE CENTRE
Broadbridge Heath Sports Centre
Wichurst Lane. Tel: (0403) 211311

TAXI
P & J Cars
80, Corsletts Avenue. Tel: (0403) 69862

GARDEN CENTRE
Three Way Stores
36 Guildford Road. Tel: (0403) 51384

🐦 🐦 🐦 🐦 🐦 🐦 🐦

BUCKS GREEN

A Wealden village between Horsham and Guildford, close to the Surrey border.

PUBLIC HOUSES
The Fox
A281. Tel: (040 372) 2386
The Queens Head
Guildford Road. Tel: (040 372) 2202

🐦 🐦 🐦 🐦 🐦 🐦 🐦

BURGESS HILL

A town right on the border between East and West Sussex. A main street connects the station and the church, with the usual collection of shops.
Population: 23,577.

RESTAURANTS

Asian Rose Authentic Tandoori
3, Keymer Parade. Tel: (0444) 232674

The China Garden
6, Mill Road. Tel: (0444) 236384

The Curry Inn Tandoori Restaurant
187, London Road. Tel: (0444) 232124

Hunters Restaurant
2, Church Road. Tel: (0444) 248874

The Indian Garden Tandoori Restaurant
199, Church Road. Tel: (0444) 246501

La Torre Italian Restaurant
171, London Road. Tel: (0444) 246889

Parisien
29/33, The Martlets. Tel: (0444) 248101

Shapla Tandoori Restaurant
226, London Road. Tel: (0444) 244771

Stalkers Restaurant
2, Keymer Road. Tel: (0444) 248210

Uncle Sams Hamburger Express
21, Station Road. Tel: (0444) 232652

PUBLIC HOUSES

Brewers Arms
London Road. Tel: (0444) 232153

Fairfield Arms
Fairfield Road. Tel: (0444) 235694

Junction Inn
Junction Road. Tel: (0444) 232311

Kings Head
London Road. Tel: (0444) 232185

The Potters Arms
129, Station Road.Tel: (0444) 233448

Railway Tavern & Burgess Brewery
Station Road. Tel: (0444) 243953

Royal George Inn
189, London Road.Tel: (0444) 233355

The Sportsman Inn
Goddards Green. Tel: (0444) 233460

The Watermill
Leyland Road. Tel: (0444) 235517

The Weald Inn
Royal George Road. Tel: (0444) 232776

The Windmill Inn
Leylands Road. Tel: (0444) 235537

The Woolpack
West Street. Tel: (0444) 241178

CAFES & TEA ROOMS

Aurora
101, Church Road. Tel: (0444) 242415

Havasnak
247, London Road. Tel: (0444) 232669

OTHER AMENITIES

BUS & COACH SERVICES
Sussex Leamland
8, Keymer Parade. Tel: (0444) 247666

CAR HIRE
Antique Executive
Tel: (0444) 247431

Burgess Hill Rent-A-Car
289, London Road. Tel: (0444) 247101

CINEMA
The Cinema
Cyprus Road. Tel: (0444) 232137

LEISURE CENTRES
Martlets Hall
The Martlets. Tel: (0444) 242888

Sheddingdean Community Centre
Maple Drive. Tel: (0444) 870154

Sidney West Centre
Leyland Road. Tel: (0444) 233168

Swimming Centre
St. Johns Park. Tel: (0444) 243735

TAXIS
A & L Taxis
94a, London Road. Tel: (0444) 870113

B.L.M. Transport
1c, Valebridge Road. Tel: (0444) 243496

Census Taxis
94a, London Road. Tel: (0444) 233501

Mid Sussex Taxis
17, Station Road. Tel: (0444) 233636

THEATRE
Malthouse Theatre Club
Scotches Farm , Malthouse Lane . Tel: (0444) 241047

🐌 🐌 🐌 🐌 🐌 🐌 🐌

BURPHAM

A very old settlement that pre-dates its near neighbour Arundel, and was a major Roman camp guarding the Arun Gap. When Arundel took over local prominence, Burpham became a tiny backwater, reached by a long winding no-through road that skirts the edge of the River Arun's floodplain, and climbs into the hillocks upon which the village sits. It has some charming houses, a busy little pub, and a mostly Norman church, St. Mary. As charming a small village as anywhere in the county.
Population: 210.

HOTEL
The Burpham Country Hotel
Old Down. Tel: (0903) 882160

PUBLIC HOUSE
The George & Dragon Inn
Tel: (0903) 883131

🐦 🐦 🐦 🐦 🐦 🐦 🐦

BURY

Bury Hill carries the main A29 up across the South Downs, and the pretty little village sits at the foot of the hill, on the other side of the River Arun to Amberley. The houses are mainly made of sandstone, and Bury House is a mock-Tudor mansion where the author of 'The Forsyte Saga', John Galsworthy, lived and died. His ashes were scattered on the downs.
Population: 637.

PUBLIC HOUSES
Black Dock & Duck Inn
The Street. Tel: (0798) 831485
The White Horse
Bury Common. Tel: (0798) 831343

OTHER AMENITY
GARDEN CENTRE
H. Bollam & Son
Hillside Nursery. Tel: (0798) 831515

🐦 🐦 🐦 🐦 🐦 🐦 🐦

BYWORTH

A tiny unspoilt village across the valley southwest of Petworth, with some pretty cottages and a popular country pub, built on the site of a 15th century priory.

PUBLIC HOUSE
Black Horse Inn
Tel: (0798) 42424

🐦 🐦 🐦 🐦 🐦 🐦 🐦

CHARLTON

A pretty, peaceful, flint-walled village at the foot of the downs just north of Goodwood, in sight of the Trundle. In the public house, The Fox Goes Free, the first ever Women's Institute meeting took place.

HOTEL
Woodstock House Hotel

Tel: (024 363) 666

PUBLIC HOUSE
Fox Goes Free Inn
Tel: (024 363) 461

🐦 🐦 🐦 🐦 🐦 🐦 🐦

THE 15TH CENTURY MARKET CROSS BUILT BY BISHOP STORY

CHICHESTER

The county town of West Sussex is an archetypal walled Roman town, based on four main streets that originally had gates; North, South, East and West Street, which all meet at the 15th century Market Cross built by Bishop Story in the middle of the town. Large chunks of the original Roman wall can be found all around this charming city, and many parts have been incorporated into the current fabric of town planning. The main streets are now 'pedestrianized', which, while making life easier for shoppers during the day, tends to rob the town of life in the evenings. The spire of the Cathedral, one of the most typical of English cathedrals, can be seen for miles around, and is the focal point for the whole of the plain between the sea and the South Downs. It dominates one side of West Street. Further down, on the other side of the street, is County Hall, headquarters of the County Council. At the top of North Street is the world-famous Chichester Festival Theatre, built to a radical design in the early Sixties, which every summer season stages four plays to packed houses. The theatre's original director was the late Sir Law-

THE SPIRE OF CHICHESTER CATHEDRAL, ONE OF THE MOST TYPICAL OF ENGLISH CATHEDRALS, CAN BE SEEN FOR MILES AROUND

rence Olivier, who set the tone and was instrumental in attracting over the years nearly every major acting talent in the country, as well as many international names. The County Court in South Street was the scene in the Sixties of the infamous trial of Rolling Stones Mick Jagger and Keith Richards for the possession of drugs, where they were initially jailed, and subsequently freed after public outcry. East Street is the major shopping street, leading from the Market Cross down to the old Corn Exchange, once the only in cinema in town, now converted into one of a hamburger chain. In the area between East and South Street are the roads called the Pallants, North, South, East and West, almost a microcosm of the city itself, full of interesting Georgian buildings, and the site of many Roman finds. The city has a bustling prosperous feel. It is a pleasant place to shop and to visit.

Population: 23,090.

PLACES OF INTEREST
Chichester Cathedral

Tel: (0243) 782595

Magnificent architecture and works of art. Site of the shrine of St Richard. Romanesque stone carvings. Famous modern paintings by Graham Sutherland, Hans Feibusch, Patrick Procktor; sculptures by John Skelton, tapestries by John Piper and Ursula Benker Schirmer; stained glass window by Marc Chagall. Situated in the heart of the city. *Months Open: All year. Days Open: Monday to Sunday. Hours Open: 7.30am-7pm summer; 5pm winter. Bank Holidays: open. Admission: Donations invited; £1 adults, 20p children.*

Chichester District Museum

Tel: (0243) 784683

Scale model of Roman Legionary. Local fossils. Roman objects from Chichester and District. City stocks on wheels. 17th Century Municipal Moon (lantern to be carried in front of the Mayor in the past). Programme of changing temporary exhibitions. Small shop. Free activity sheets for children. *Months Open: All year. Days Open: Tuesday to Saturday. Hours Open: 10am-5.30pm. Admission: free. Displays tell story of Chichester district - geology, archaeology and local history.*

Guildhall Museum
Tel: (0243) 784683

HOTELS
Bedford Hotel
Southgate. Tel: (0243) 785766
Chichester Resort Hotel
16 Chichester Road. Tel: (Freephone 0800) 500 100
Dolphin & Anchor Hotel
West Street. Tel: (0243) 785121
The Globe Hotel
1 Southgate. Tel: (0243) 782035/785607
The Nags Head Hotel
2 St. Pancras. Tel: (0243) 785823
The Ship Hotel
57 North Street. Tel: (0243) 782028
The Suffolk House Hotel
3 East Row. Tel: (0243) 778899

GUEST HOUSES
Ashby's Guest House
23 Stockbridge Road. Tel: (0243) 786227
N.D. Mackintosh
12 The Avenue. Tel: (0243) 527135
Willow Cottage
100 Fishbourne Road. Tel: (0243) 785874

RESTAURANTS
Akash Tandoori Restaurant
Old Swimming Pool, Eastgate Square. Tel: (0243) 775978/779845
Al's Diner
9 Almhouse Arcade, 19 The Hornet. Tel: (0243) 783045
Chichester Tandoori Indian Restaurant
5/6 South Street. Tel: (0243) 785764
Clinch's Salad House
14 Southgate. Tel: (0243) 788822
Comme Ca
149 St. Pancras. Tel: (0243) 788724
Confucius Chinese Restaurant
2 Cooper Street. Tel: (0243) 783158/783790

Crusties
10 Crane Street. Tel: (0243) 533620
Dragon Spring
81 East Street. Tel: (0243) 785631
Fillers
4 West Street. Tel: (0243) 771631
Flints Brasserie
St. Peters Market, West Street. Tel: (0243) 531611/2
Giuliano's Restaurant
117 St. Pancras. Tel: (0243) 784232
Happy Palace
31a Southgate. Tel: (0243) 781613
Indian Cottage Restaurant
The Old Tollgate, Westgate. Tel: (0243) 780859
The Jasmin House
28 The Hornet. Tel: (0243) 786719
Lotus Garden Chinese Take Away
48 North Street. Tel: (0243) 782587
McDonald's Hamburgers
Corn Exchange, East Street. Tel: (0243) 778149
Micawber's Kitchen
13 South Street. Tel: (0243) 786989
Nicodemus Restaurant
14 St. Pancras. Tel: (0243) 787521
Noble Rot Brasserie & Wine Bar
3 Little London. Tel: (0243) 779922
Two hundred year old wine cellars within the city walls provide the perfect setting for this lively brasserie.
Specialities: Giant flat field mushrooms, deep fried brie, chicken in tarragon, veal dijonnaise. Open 11.00-11.00pm. Last Orders: 11.00pm. Lunch: £ 4.50. Dinner: £ 10.00. House Wine: £ 5.95. Credit Cards: Ac. Am. D. V. Seating Capacity: 65. Veg. B. P. W.
The Old Cross
65 North Street. Tel: (0243) 785029
Parklands Fish Bar
1 The Ridgeway. Tel: (0243) 783468
Pasta in the Park
The Park Tavern, 11 Priory Road. Tel: (0243) 785057
The Perfect Blend
17 Sadlers Walk, East Street. Tel: (0243) 776013
Perfect Pizza
36 The Hornet. Tel: (0243) 533033
Pizza Express
27 South Street. Tel: (0243) 786648
Pop's Choice
26 North Street. Tel: (0243) 782078
Sadlers Wine Bar & Restaurant
42 East Street. Tel: (0243) 774765
Sealand Fish Bar
110 The Hornet. Tel: (0243) 775454
St. Martins Tea Rooms
3 St. Martins Street. Tel: (0243) 786715
St. Pancras Fish Bar
78 St. Pancras. Tel: (0243) 783254

Sweeny Todd's
Vicars Hall, South Street. Tel: (0243) 784794

The Terrace Restaurant
11 Priory Road. Tel: (0243) 786543

Thirteen Southgate
13 Southgate. Tel: (0243) 776634

Thompson's Restaurant
30a Southgate. Tel: (0243) 528832

Through the Greenhouse
24 St. Pancras. Tel: (0243) 788814

Uncle Sam's Hamburger Express
The Bus Station, Southgate. Tel: (0243) 531648

Wheeler's Restaurants plc
38 Little London. Tel: (0243) 784899

Whyke Fisheries
3 Hardham Road. Tel: (0243) 783444

Woodies Wine Bar
10-11 St. Pancras. Tel: (0243) 779895

PUBLIC HOUSES

The Barley Mow
101 Oving Road. Tel: (0243) 784708

Black Horse Inn
Birdham Road. Tel: (0243) 784068

The Bull Inn
4/5 Market Road. Tel: (0243) 785301

The Bush Inn
The Hornet. Tel: (0243) 779945

The Castle Inn
38 West Street. Tel: (0243) 783185

Cathedral Tavern
29 Southgate. Tel: (0243) 781352

Chequers Inn
203 Oving Road. Tel: (0243) 786427

The Coach & Horses
125 St. Pancras. Tel: (0243) 787262

Crown Inn
Whyke Road. Tel: (0243) 785009

The Eastergate Inn
4 The Hornet. Tel: (0243) 774877

The Four Chestnuts
Oving Road. Tel: (0243) 779974

George & Dragon
51 North Street. Tel: (0243) 785660

The Hole in the Wall
St. Martins Street. Tel: (0243) 782555

Kings Head
5 South Street. Tel: (0243) 785753

The Mitre
Oliver Whitby Road. Tel: (0243) 785942

New Inn
35 Whyke Road. Tel: (0243) 782238

The Old House at Home
145 Broyle Road. Tel: (0243) 781623

The Park Tavern
11 Priory Road. Tel: (0243) 785057

Rainbow Tavern
56 St. Pauls Road. Tel: (0243) 785867
*Brewery: Ind Coope. Licensee: Mr Keith Dixon. OPEN ALL
DAY. Beer available: Traditional cask conditioned ales. Food
available: All day.*

The Richmond Arms
9 Stockbridge Road. Tel: (0243) 785873

Royal Arms
92 East Street. Tel: (0243) 782148

Ye Old Sussex Barn
99 Fishbourne Road. Tel: (0243) 785707

The Swan
12 Westgate. Tel: (0243) 785044

The Victoria
24 St. Pancras. Tel: (0243) 779913

The Wallington Inn
67 Broyle Road. Tel: (0243) 782286

Wheatsheaf Inn
Oving Road. Tel: (0243) 785021

The White Horse
South Street. Tel: (0243) 785804

The Wickham Arms
Bognor Road. Tel: (0243) 784782

The Woolpack Inn
71 Fishbourne Road. Tel: (0243) 782792

CAFES & TEA ROOMS

The Crooked S
North Street. Tel: (0243) 780365

End of the Lane
Unit 6 Jay Walk, St. Martins Street. Tel: (0243) 531135

Flints Brasserie
St. Peters Market, West Street. Tel: (0243) 531611/531612

C.R. Jewer
Chichester Bus Station, Southgate. Tel: (0243) 785646

Lizza Pizza
St. Johns Street. Tel: (0243) 533467

The Lunch Box
20 Butter Market, North Street. Tel: (0243) 788492

D. Morelli
66 East Street. Tel: (0243) 782392

Oki-Doki's Coffee House
30b Southgate. Tel: (0243) 532427

The Primrose Cafe
11 Adelaide Road. Tel: (0243) 785087

Shepherds Tea Rooms
35 Little London. Tel: (0243) 774761

OTHER AMENITIES

ART GALLERIES

The Canon Gallery

24 South Street. Tel: (0243) 786063
Chichester Picture Gallery
Upper Shopping Centre, Butter Market, North Street.
Tel: (0243) 784836
Crane Galleries
4a Crane Street. Tel: (0243) 782226
David Paul Gallery
27 The Hornet. Tel: (0243) 783677
Hornblower Gallery
Unit 25 Sadlers Walk, 44 East Street. Tel: (0243) 531316
Nigel Purchase Gallery
11 The Hornet. Tel: (0243) 782018
Chichester Centre of Arts Ltd.
St. Andrews Court, East Street. Tel: (0243) 779103
Pallant House Gallery
9 North Pallant. Tel: (0243) 774557

BUS & COACH SERVICES
Southdown Motor Services
Bus Station, Southgate. Tel: (0243) 783251

CAR HIRE/CHAUFFEUR DRIVE
Central of Chichester
Kiosk, Northside, Railway Approach. PO19 2DN Tel:
(0243) 782377
Dunnaway's
3 Little London. Tel: (0243) 782403/789136

CAR HIRE/SELF DRIVE
Autorent [Whyke Motors Ltd.]
Bognor Road. Tel: (0243) 787684
City Hire
Terminus Road, Industrial Estate. Tel: (0243) 776622
Europcar [D. Rowe & Co. Ltd.]
The Hornet. Tel: (0243) 78810
Whyke Autorent
51 Bognor Road. Tel: (0243) 775538

FLORISTS
Brentons of Chichester
10 Southgate. Tel: (0243) 781814
Chichester Flowers
46 The Hornet. Tel: (0243) 786977
The Flower Shop
16 Sadlers Walk, 44 East Street. Tel: (0243) 775577
Hoopers of Chichester
14 South Street. Tel: (0243) 786341
The Silk Greenhouse
12 Priory Lane, Northgate. Tel: (0243) 532227

GARDEN CENTRES
D. Combes
Thatched Barn, 51 The Hornet. Tel: (0243) 781445
Elfords

Unit 4 Benturner Industrial Estate, Oving Road. Tel:
(0243) 787721

HEALTH CLUBS
Body Sense Chichester
26a The Hornet. Tel: (0243) 774792
Health & Beauty Body Tuning Salon
Months Open: 12. Days Open: Monday to Friday and Saturday
morning. Hours Open: 8.30am-9pm. Body toning and slim-
ming. Full beauty services include waxing, facials, electrolysis,
manicures, eyebrow shaping etc. Plus health and fitness. Man-
ager: Mr Malcolm Butcher.
Profiles
The Old Granary, Northgate. Tel: (0243) 774793
Health Club
Months Open: All. Days Open: Monday to Sunday. Hours
Open: 9am to 10pm Monday to Friday, 9am to 4pm Saturday,
10am-4pm Sunday. Manager: Mr Ray Evans.

LEISURE CENTRE
Westgate Leisure Centre
Avenue De Chartres. Tel: (0243) 785651
Leisure Centre
Months Open: All. Days Open: Monday to Sunday. Hours
Open: Monday 10am - 10.30pm, Tuesday - Saturday 7.30am -
10.30pm, Sunday 9am - 6pm. Bank Holidays: Open every
holiday except Christmas Day, Boxing Day, New Years Day.
Sports hall, creche, restaurant, swimming pools, conditioning
room, activities room, sports clinic, squash courts, cafeteria,
licensed bar, water slide (40m), health suite: 2 sunbeds, sauna,
steam room, beauty salon. Manager: Mr G Mayhew.

LIBRARY
Chichester Central Library
Tower Street. Tel: (0243) 777351

MARINA
St. Georges Marina
Sussex Suite, 2/4 Southgate. Tel: (0243) 774490

SNOOKER CENTRES
Chichester Snooker Club
The Old Mill, Terminus Road. Tel: (0243) 531830
The Triangle Club
1 St. Pancras. Tel: (0243) 782977

STORES
Army & Navy
St. Georges House, West Street. Tel: (0243) 786551
Hoopers
St. Peters House, North Street. PO19 1LT Tel: (0243)
533103
Marks & Spencer plc
16 East Street. Tel: (0243) 782598/787452

TAXIS
Cabicar
82 Fishbourne Road. Tel: (0243) 776288/780517
Central Taxis
Railway Station Approach. Tel: (0243) 789432/782377
Taxi & Chauffeur Car Services
Days Open: Every day. Hours Open: 24 hours. Proprietor: Mr
F Wallbridge.
City Cabs (Chichester)
Tenacre Close. Tel: (0243) 775946
J. Dunnaway Car Hire
The Taxi Terminal, 3 Little London. Tel: (0243) 782403/
789136
Ladyline Taxis
50 Somerstown. Tel: (0243) 531103

THEATRE
Chichester Festival Theatre
Oaklands Park. PO19 4AP Tel: (0243) 781312

WATER SPORTS
Windsurfing Imports
7 Angel Industrial Units, Quarry Lane Industrial Estate.
Tel: (0243) 786056

🐾 🐾 🐾 🐾 🐾 🐾 🐾

CHIDHAM
A totally unspoilt scattered village on a spit of land in Chichester Harbour, situated on a cul-de-sac off the Chichester-Portsmouth road, across an inlet from Bosham. Pretty houses, barns and church.
Population: 902.

PUBLIC HOUSE
Old House at Home
Cot Lane. Tel: (0243) 572447

OTHER AMENITY
GARDEN CENTRE
Greenacre Nursery
Main Road. Tel: (0243) 572441

🐾 🐾 🐾 🐾 🐾 🐾 🐾

CHILGROVE
A tiny rural hamlet on the Chichester-Petersfield road, set in a fold in the downs. This whole area was the Romans' wheat basin. A large green in front of the White Horse is a popular picnic spot.

RESTAURANTS
The Hideaway Restaurant
The Royal Oak, Hooksway. Tel: (024 359) 257

The White Horse Inn
High Street. Tel: (024 359) 251
Fully licensed free house and restaurant set in the glorious South Downs between Chichester and Petersfield.
English and French Cuisine. Specialities: Lobster , Crab, Game. Hours Open: Lunch: 12.00-3.00. Dinner: 7.00-12.00. Last Orders: 9.30. Closed Sunday evening and all day Monday. Open for lunch Sundays. Lunch: £ 15.00. Dinner: £ 20.00. House Wine: £ 7.95. Credit Cards: Ac. V. Seats 70. Outdoor Eating. Veg. W/Chair. P. W. Recommended: AA. ER. M.

PUBLIC HOUSE
The Royal Oak
Hooksway. Tel: (024 359) 257

🐾 🐾 🐾 🐾 🐾 🐾 🐾

CLAPHAM
A pleasant village on the slopes of the downs just off the main A27 coast road. There is a common, very different in nature to its namesake in London, and an Early English church, St Mary.
Population: 324.

PUBLIC HOUSES
Anchor Inn
80, High Street.
The Swan Inn
79, High Street.Tel: (0903) 32923

🐾 🐾 🐾 🐾 🐾 🐾 🐾

CLAYTON
A village north of the downs above Brighton, remarkable for its two windmills, Jack and Jill, and for the unique castellated entrance to the railway tunnel.

PUBLIC HOUSE
The Jack And Jill Inn
Brighton Road. Tel: (079 18) 3595

CLIMPING

A tiny rural village scattered along the one lane that leads down to the sea. The coastline here, to the mouth of the Arun, and Littlehampton beyond, is entirely untouched, the only stretch between Selsey Bill and Brighton so to be. There are wild, unkempt sand-dunes, leading down to a vast expanse of beach free of the ubiquitous breakwaters. The dunes are the habitat of some nudists, and the occasional film-maker who wishes to recreate Normandy Beach without having to go there. Bailiffscourt, now a hotel, is an architectural curiosity. Built on the site of 13th century chapel in 1935 by Lord Moyne, the building is in fact a reproduction of a medieval house built around a square courtyard, with barns and cottages around.
Population: 830.

HOTEL
Bailiffscourt Hotel & Restaurant
Climping Street. Tel: (0903) 723511

PUBLIC HOUSE
The Black Horse
Climping Street. Tel: (0903) 715175

OTHER AMENITIES
CARAVAN PARK
Sevenacres Caravan Park
Horsemere Green Lane. Tel: (0903) 713604

GARDEN CENTRE
Ford Acres Nursery
Horsemere Green Lane. Tel: (0903) 716637

COATES

A remote village in the Weald south of Petworth, with some pretty cottages and the manor house grouped around the church, St. Agatha.

PLACES OF INTEREST
Coates Manor
Shrubs and foliage of special interest
Days Open: June 17, 18, 19. Hours Open: 11-6pm. Admission: £1.00; children 20p. Also open by appointment.

COCKING

At the bottom of Cocking Hill, between Midhurst and Chichester, Cocking nestles beneath the South Downs. Mainly grouped along the main street,

many of the cottages bear the distinctive yellow paint of the Cowdray Estate.
Population: 439.

HOTEL
The Potter & Vine
Tel: (073 081) 3449

PUBLIC HOUSE
The Richard Cobden Inn
Tel: (073 081) 2974

OTHER AMENITY
TAXI
Midhurst Taxis
41 The Croft. Tel: (073 081) 3988

COLDWALTHAM

An unremarkable village straggling along the main A29 south of Pulborough.
Population: 816.

RESTAURANTS
The Barn Owls
Tel: (079 82) 2498
The Old Priest House
Tel: (079 82) 2694

COMPTON

A delightful downland village of flint and brick close to the Hampshire border, centred around the convergence of three roads, where the village shop and pub are. St. Mary's church stands beneath the slope of Telegraph Hill, at 533 feet, beyond which is the Neolithic Long Barrow known as Bevis's Thumb.
Population: 418.

PUBLIC HOUSE
The Coach & Horses
The Square. Tel: (0705) 631228

COOLHAM

The quaintly named 'Blue Idol' Quaker meeting-house here was frequented by William Penn (founder of Pennsylvania) who lived at nearby Warminghurst.

GUEST HOUSE
Blue Idol Guest House
Old House Lane. Tel: (040 387) 241

PUBLIC HOUSE
The Selsey Arms
Tel: (040 387) 537

OTHER AMENITY
CARAVAN PARK
Brook Green Caravan Park
Tel: (040 387) 507
Proprietor: R.B.F. Morris.

⁊⁊ ⁊⁊ ⁊⁊ ⁊⁊ ⁊⁊ ⁊⁊ ⁊⁊

COPTHORNE
A village very close to the Surrey broder, northeast of Crawley. The architect George Smith built the house 'Newlands' for himself in 1848.

HOTEL
The Copthorne
Copthorne Road. RH10 3PQ. Tel: (0342) 714971

RESTAURANT
Alexanders
Fen Place, Turners Hill. Tel: (0342) 714914

OTHER AMENITIES
CAR HIRE
AI Fullers International
The Copthorne Hotel. Tel: (0342) 716456
Crest Cars
Effingham Road. Tel: (0342) 714195

⁊⁊ ⁊⁊ ⁊⁊ ⁊⁊ ⁊⁊ ⁊⁊ ⁊⁊

COWFOLD
A truly picturesque village between Horsham and the downs. The houses and cottages are built of brick, tile and weatherboard.
Population: 1,259.

PUBLIC HOUSES
Hare & Hounds
Henfield Road. Tel: (0403) 864376
The Red Lion
Horsham Road. Tel: (0403) 864247

CAFE/TEA ROOMS
Chalet Cafe
Brighton Road. Tel: (0403) 864314

OTHER AMENITY
CAR HIRE
Antique & Executive Car Hire
Littlebrook Horsham Road. Tel: (0403) 864443

⁊⁊ ⁊⁊ ⁊⁊ ⁊⁊ ⁊⁊ ⁊⁊ ⁊⁊

CRAWLEY
One of the New Towns created after the Second World War, 1947, Crawley actually embraces ten existing settlements. Clockwise, they are Northgate, Lowfield Heath, Three Bridges, Pound Hill, Southgate, Tilgate, West Green, Gossops Green, Ifield, and Langley Green. The proximity of Gatwick Airport provides work for many, as do the industrial estates, well separated from the residential parts of the town. Open spaces have been well utilised to lessen the worst effects of high-density housing, and the overall planning of Crawley, for a New Town, is not without success.

HOTELS
Crest Hotels
Langley Drive. Tel: (0293) 29991
The George Hotel
High Street. Tel: (0293) 24215
Goffs Park Hotel
Goffs Park Road. Tel: (0293) 35447
The Grange Hotel
15, Brighton Road. Tel: (0293) 35191

GUEST HOUSES
Doeswood Guest House
1, London Road. Tel: (0293) 31558
Ferndale Guest house
124, Malthouse Road. Tel: (0293) 20368
Porsh
44 Alpha Road, West Green. Tel: (0293) 551122

RESTAURANTS
The Coffee Shop Kebab House
4, The Broadwalk. Tel: (0293) 545496
The Golden Griddle Restaurant
Tel: (0293) 36961
Good Fortune Chinese Restaurant
98, High Street. Tel: (0293) 20432
Good View
31, The Martlets. Tel: (0293) 22521
The James King
Tel: (0293) 27140
Lastrada Restaurant
60, High Street. Tel: (0293) 543744
Mansing Cantonese Restaurant
213, Three Bridges Road. Tel: (0293) 548041

31

McDonalds
24, Haslett Avenue. Tel: (0293) 546277
Mithali Tandoori Restaurant
27, The Broadway. Tel: (0293) 546499
The Piazza Continental Restaurant
5, Broadwalk. Tel: (0293) 23641
The Rendezvous
58, Boulevard. Tel: (0293) 22495
Solomon's Ancient Prior Restaurant & Wine Bar
49, High Street. Tel: (0293) 36223
Sparks Fast Foods
22, High Street. Tel: (0293) 25856/551138
Taj Mahal Restaurant
4, High Street. Tel: (0293) 29755/26197
Wimpy Restaurant
7, Martletts. Tel: (0293) 36573

PUBLIC HOUSES
Brewery Shades
High Street. Tel: (0293) 514105
Crown Inn
Ifield Road. Tel: (0293) 20636
The Greyhound
Tinsley Green. Tel: (0293) 884220
Hoppers
Ashdown Drive, Tilgate.Tel: (0293) 510768
Inn in the Park
Tilgate Park, Tilgate Drive.Tel: (0293) 545324
Maid of Sussex
Gales Drive. Tel: (0293) 25404
The Mark Lemon Public House
Broadfield Barton. Tel: (0293) 26237
Moonraker
199, Three Bridges Road.Tel: (0293) 35896
Parsons Pig
Black Corner, Balcombe Road.Tel: (0293) 883104
Pelhams
Ifield Drive. Tel: (0293) 25412
The Plough
181, Three Bridges Road.Tel: (0293) 24487
Sun Hotel
High Street. Tel: (0293) 20030
Swan Inn
1 Horsham Road, West Gardens.Tel: (0293) 27447
The White Hart
Tel: (0293) 20033
The Windmill
Gossops Drive, Gossops Green.Tel: (0293) 26289

CAFES & TEA ROOMS
American Beefburger Bar
38, The Broadway. Tel: (0293) 544425
Bretts Cafe
8, Langley Parade. Tel: (0293) 23707

OTHER AMENITIES
BUS & COACH SERVICES
Flightlink
Terminal Buildings, Gatwick Airport. Tel: (0293) 514244
London Country Bus
Bus Station , Haslett Avenue. Tel: (0293) 25173

CAR HIRE
Avis Rent-A-Car
Gatwick Airport. Tel: (0293) 29721
Budget Rent-A-Car
International Arrivals Hall , Gatwick Airport. Tel: (0293) 540141
Century Self Drive
Room 9 Grange Hotel , 15 Brighton Road. Tel: (0293) 560961
Fieldale
Overdene Drive. Tel: (0293) 515551
Gatwick Rent-A-Car
24, Ash Keys. Tel: (0293) 512247
Guy Salmon Car Rentals
Crest Hotel, Langley Drive. Tel: (0293) 547671
K. F. Cars
Concorde House, Gatwick Airport. Tel: (0293) 514621
Kenning Car & Van Rental
Manor Royal Service Station , Gatwick Road. Tel: (0293) 514822
Kingsfold Rolls Royce Hire Company
Unit 5, Forge Wood Ind. Est. , Gatwick Road. Tel: (0293) 558684/548685
Surrey & Sussex Self Drive
14, Priestley Way. Tel: (0293) 553458
Tristar Cars
Black Corner Garage , Balcombe Road. Tel: (0293) 26001
Windwill Garage
Old Brighton Road , Lowefield Heath. Tel: (0293) 513031

CARAVAN PARK
Amberley Fields Caravan Club
Charlwood Road , Lowefield Heath. Tel: (0293) 24834

GARDEN CENTRES
Cheals Garden Centre
Horsham Road. Tel: (0293) 22101
Gledhow Farm Nursery
Sreers Lane , Tinsley Green. Tel: (0293) 884077
Wakehams Green Garden Centre
Tel: (0293) 882413
Windmill Nurseries
Copthorne Road. Tel: (0293) 886007

HEALTH CLUB
Allington Health Club

Gatwick Airport. Tel: (0293) 27261

LEISURE CENTRE
Crawley Leisure Centre
Haslett Avenue. Tel: (0293) 374431

SAUNA
Sun Dial Leisure Services
176, Weald Drive. Tel: (0293) 516425

STORES
Alders International
Gatwick Airport. Tel: (0293) 502029
Co-Operative Retail Services
14 - 26, The Broadway. Tel: (0293) 25731
Littlewoods Organisation Plc
1 - 5, Queensway. Tel: (0293) 30404
Marks & Spencer Plc.
23, Queensway. Tel: (0293) 549061
Woolworths Plc
17, Queens Square. Tel: (0293) 516396/25401

TAXIS
Barker G & Sons
198, Haslett Avenue. Tel: (0293) 24151
Crawley Taxis & Cars
Crawley Station , Station Way. Tel: (0293) 35555
Goldline Taxis
1, East Park. Tel: (0293) 551515
Mascot Car Hire
Tel: (0293) 34600
Phoenix Cars
32, High Street. Tel: (0293) 544571
Ranks
Crawley Station. Tel: (0293) 37177

🐦 🐦 🐦 🐦 🐦 🐦 🐦

CROCKER HILL
A small collection of houses, a garage, a pub, latterly turned right around by the creation of a new section of the main A27 by-passing the place.

PUBLIC HOUSE
The Winterton Arms
Tel: (0243) 773202

🐦 🐦 🐦 🐦 🐦 🐦 🐦

CUCKFIELD
A large, old village immediately west of Haywards Heath, that began life as a Norman hunting-lodge and chapel. On the outskirts of the town is a sign with a cuckoo, hinting at the origin of the

HOUSES IN CUCKFIELD

Saxon name 'Cucufelda', meaning 'a clearing of cuckoos'. Built on the side of a hill, there is a pretty High Street, and some fine historical houses, including an early 17th century timber-framed house, now a hotel.

PLACES OF INTEREST
Cuckfield Museum
Queen's Hall, High Street.
Inaugurated in 1980 the museum is mostly concerned with the village of Cuckfield and the mid-Sussex area. Covers local history, local records and photographs, postcards and maps, paintings, ceramics, costumes, toys and archaeological items.
Months Open: Mid March - Mid January. Days Open: Tuesday, Wednesday and Saturday or by arrangement. Hours Open: 10am-12.30pm. Bank Holidays: 2pm-5pm. Admission: free.

HOTELS
The Hilton Park Hotel
Tylers Green. Tel: (0444) 454555
The Kings Head Hotel
South Street. RH17 5JY. Tel: (0444) 454006
Ockenden Manor Hotel
Ockenden Lane. Tel: (0444) 41611
The Wheatsheaf Hotel
Broad Street. Tel: (0444) 454078

RESTAURANTS
Clouseaus Restaurant
1, Ockenden Lane. Tel: (0444) 450536
Jeremy's Restaurant
Tel: (0444) 440386
Murrays Restaurant
White Cottage, Broad Street. Tel: (0444) 455826

PUBLIC HOUSES
Rose & Crown Inn

33

DELL QUAY, A CHARMING YACHTING CENTRE ON CHICHESTER HARBOUR

London Road. Tel: (0444) 454046
The Ship Inn
Whitemans Green. Tel: (0444) 413219
The Talbot Inn
High Street. Tel: (0444) 413137
The White Harte Inn
South Street. Tel: (0444) 413454

🐚 🐚 🐚 🐚 🐚 🐚 🐚

DELL QUAY

A charming yachting centre on Chichester Harbour which was the main port for Chichester from the 17th century until the canal was built.

PUBLIC HOUSE
Crown & Anchor
Tel: (0243) 781712

OTHER AMENITIES
BOAT MOORINGS
Ted Bailey & Co
Dell Quay Yacht Yard, Dell Quay Road. Tel: (0243) 785954

GARDEN CENTRE
Apuldram Roses
Apuldram Lane. PO20 7EF Tel: (0243) 785769
Rose nursery

Months Open: All year. Days Open: Monday to Sunday. Hours Open: 9am - 5pm, Sunday 10.30 - 4.30. Bank Holidays: 10.30 - 4.30. 250 varieties of roses, hybrid teas, floribundas, climbers, ramblers, miniatures, patio, ground cover, old-fashioned and modern shrubs. Proprietor: Mrs D Sawday.

🐚 🐚 🐚 🐚 🐚 🐚 🐚

DIAL POST

A strangely-named village that straggles along the A24 road between Horsham and Worthing.

RESTAURANTS
Basing Cottage
Tel: (0903) 892322
The Peppermill
35, Worthing Road. Tel: (0403) 710246
A very light & spacious restaurant with a friendly atmosphere overlooking our picturesque gardens. English & French Cuisine. Specialities: All dishes home made from fresh local produce. Hours Open: Lunch: 12.00-1.30. Dinner: 7.00. Last Orders: 10.00. Closed All day Monday & Tuesday lunch. Open Sundays. Lunch: £ 9.25. Dinner: £ 14.95. House Wine: £ 6.25. Credit Cards: Ac. Am. D. V. Seating Capacity: 60. Outdoor eating. N/S areas. Veg. W/Chair. B. P. W.

PUBLIC HOUSE
Crown Inn
Worthing Road. Tel: (0403) 710902

ONE OF THE SUPERB HALF-TIMBERED HOUSES AT EASEBOURNE (PAGE 36)

DUNCTON

A small village on the main road between Pet-worth and Chichester, mostly renowned for its steep hill up the downs that has provedtoo much for many an ancient banger with its steep incline, and its hairpin bends. Seaford College, a boys' public school, and St Michael's girls' school both occupy fine old buildings.
Population: 298.

PUBLIC HOUSE
Cricketer Arms
Chichester Road. Tel: (0798) 42473

OTHER AMENITY
FISH FARM
Duncton Mill Trout Farm & Hatchery
Duncton Mill. Tel: (0798) 42048

EARNLEY

A village on the western side of the Selsey penin-sular, half a mile from the coast. The 13th century church stands on a triangle in the centre of the village. Earnley has been somewhat absorbed by its neighbour Bracklesham and the coastal con-

structions, but is still recognizable as a group.
Population: 260.

OTHER AMENITIES
GARDEN CENTRE
Garden Care of Earnley
Almodington Lane. Tel: (0243) 512637

HOLIDAY CAMP
Sussex Beach Holiday Village
PO20 7JP Tel: (0243) 671213

EARTHAM

A small unspoilt rural village on the wooded slopes north-east of Chichester, composed of some attrac-tive flint cottages, a small Norman church and a popular pub. Nearby at Eartham Wood an original section of Stane Street cuts through Forestry Commission land, north to Bignor Hill. A lovely walk, the original mound or 'agger' of the road is well preserved.

PUBLIC HOUSE
The George Inn
Tel: (024 365) 340

35

STANDEN, EAST GRINSTEAD, OWNED BY THE NATIONAL TRUST

EASEBOURNE

Connecting Midhurst and Cowdray Park, Easebourne is almost entirely owned by the Cowdray Estate, and has some superb half-timbered houses, some painted in the distinctive yellow. Easebourne Priory, founded in the early 13th century, is now a private house, attached to the much-restored church, St Mary.

Population: 1,924.

PUBLIC HOUSES

Holly Tree Inn
Easebourne Street. Tel: (073 081) 3388
The White Horse
Easebourne Street. Tel: (073 081) 3521

🐾 🐾 🐾 🐾 🐾 🐾 🐾

EAST ASHLING

Paired with West Ashling, a hamlet in the flat wooded area north-west of Chichester, mainly grouped along the road.

PUBLIC HOUSE

The Horse & Groom
Tel: (0243) 575339

OTHER AMENITY

GARDEN CENTRE
East Ashling Nurseries
Lye Lane. Tel: (0243) 575523

🐾 🐾 🐾 🐾 🐾 🐾 🐾

EAST DEAN

Not to be confused with Eastdean in East Sussex, this village is in the Lavant valley that runs east—west beneath the South Downs, with some pretty flint and half-timbered houses built around a duck-

pond. The Star and Garter pub sign bears the legend 'Honi soit qui mal y pense', loosely translated as 'evil be to him who evil thinks', referring to King Charles' utterance when he created the order of the garter. An excellent centre for walking.

Population: 237.

PUBLIC HOUSE

The Star & Garter
Tel: (024 363) 318

🐾 🐾 🐾 🐾 🐾 🐾 🐾

EAST GRINSTEAD

The name of this commuter town means 'clearing in the woodland', and was once just that when Ashdown Forest was much more extensive than it is now. Although when approached from any direction East Grinstead seems to be a collection of housing estates, the heart of the town is essentially Tudor, with many half-timbered buildings, and a church, St Swithun, rebuilt in the 18th century, which stands on an ancient site. The town has long been a centre for pioneering work in plastic surgery, based at Queen Victoria Hospital, and there are associations with cult religions; the Mormons have their headquarters here, there is a Buddhist retreat, and the Scientologists are based here.

Population: 22,054.

PLACES OF INTEREST

East Grinstead Town Museum
East Court.
Tel: (0342) 322511
Local history including craft bygones (notably pottery). Temporary exhibitions, changed quarterly (1990 April-June Heraldry, July-Sept Postal History, Oct-Dec Framed Buildings of the Weald).
Months Open: All year round. Days Open: Wednesday and Saturday. Hours Open: 2-4pm (2-5pm Saturdays April - October). Bank Holidays: as announced. Admission: Free. Stairs difficult for disabled people. Private parties outside normal hours by arrangement.

Hammerwood Park
Tel: (0342) 850594
Set in picturesque Sussex landscape, Hammerwood Park was built in 1792 by Latrobe, architect of the White House and The Capitol, Washington DC. Extensive restoration works have been completed and won numerous awards.

Monthly concerts are given. Additional exhibitions: 150 years of photography; costume - love & marriage. Copy of the Elgin Marbles.
Months Open: Easter Monday to end of September. Days Open: Wednesdays, Saturdays and Bank Holiday Mondays. Hours Open: 2pm-5.30pm. Admission: £2.50. Children £1.25. Tours and luscious cream teas.

Standen
A house designed by Philip Webb with a fine collection of William Morris designed soft furnishings. Beautiful gardens with stunning views across the Medway Valley. Tel: (0342) 23029
Months Open: April to end October. Days Open: Wed to Sun. Hours Open: Restaurant & garden 1-5.30pm; house 1.30-5.30pm. Bank Holidays: Open Bank Holiday Mondays. Admission: £2.80; garden only £1.40. Children half price.

HOTELS

Acorn Lodge Hotel
Turners Hill Road. Tel: (0342) 323207

Cranfield Lodge Hotel
Maypole Road. RH19 1HW. Tel: (0342)321251

Cranston House
Cranston Road. Tel: (0342)323609

The Crown
High Street. Tel: (0342) 323117

Felbridge Hotel
London Road. Tel: (0342) 326992

Gravetye Manor Hotel
Vowels Lane. Tel: (0342) 810567

Victoria Bed & Breakfast
17 Portland Road. Tel: (0342) 322308

Woodbury Hotel
Lewes Road. Tel: (0342) 313657

RESTAURANTS

Anne Tree Restaurant
61 High Street. Tel: (0342) 321976

Z. Bedir
6 Railway Approach. Tel: (0342) 410305

Chadbergers
22 Railway Approach. Tel: (0342) 321575

China Chef
108 London Road. Tel: (0342) 312244

The Coach House Inn
Wilderwick Road. Tel: (034 287) 448

The Corner Steak House
31 High Street. Tel: (0342) 321448

Curry House
186 London Road. Tel: (0342) 325267

Dixieland Fried Chicken
184 London Road. Tel: (0342) 326640

Dorset Arms
High Street. Tel: (0342) 321797

Dunnings Mill Restaurant
Dunnings Road. Tel: (0342) 326341

Evergreen Restaurant
192 London Road. Tel: (0342) 322078

La Farola Restaurant
194 London Road. Tel: (0342) 322399

La Zingara
125 London Road. Tel: (0342) 324541

Monsoon Indian Restaurant
51 High Street. Tel: (0342) 324449/314576

Mr Chippy
45 Holtye Avenue. Tel: (0342) 328568

Nizam Tandoori
42 High Street. Tel: (0342) 314652

Shapla Tandoori Restaurant & Takeaway
94 Railway Approach. Tel: (0342) 327655/327663

Taylors Fish Bar
18 Railway Approach. Tel: (0342) 321587

Telephone Pizza Company
32 Railway Approach. Tel: (0342) 410734

Wimpy Restaurant
78-86, London Road. Tel: (0342) 323267

Wing-Wah Chinese Restaurant
195 London Road. Tel: (0342) 324343

PUBLIC HOUSES

The Guinea Pig
Holtye Rise. Tel: (0342) 323704

Prince of Wales
Lingfield Road. Tel: (0342) 325703

Rose & Crown
65 High Street. Tel: (0342) 322176

The Ship Inn
Ship Street. Tel: (0342) 323197

Sussex Arms
West Street. Tel: (0342) 323110

The White Lion
London Road. Tel: (0342) 323356

OTHER AMENITIES

CAR HIRE

Frobishers Limousine Services
77 London Road. RH19 1EQ Tel: (0342) 315556/316280

Autorent
Sidlow Garage, London Road. Tel: (0342) 315722

Fona-Van
67 Railway Approach. Tel: (0342) 323681

GARDEN CENTRE

Orchard Nursery
Holtye Road. Tel: (0342) 311657

HOSPITAL

Queen Victoria Hospital

Commonwealth House, Holtye Road. Tel: (0342) 322688

LEISURE CENTRE
Kings Centre
Moat Road. Tel: (0342) 328616

NIGHT CLUB
Martines Night Club
The Whitehall, London Road. Tel: (0342) 322197

SNOOKER CENTRE
Dunnings Mill Snooker Club
Dunnings Road. Tel: (0342) 314217

STORE
Woolworths plc
22 London Road. Tel: (0342) 322170

TAXIS
A1 Taxis
3 The Close, Brooklands Way. Tel: (0342) 313833
Acorn Cars
15 Meadowcroft Close. Tel: (0342) 410518
E.G. Cars
213-217 London Road. Tel: (0342) 410808
Fonacar Private Hire
67 Railway Approach. Tel: (0342) 321010
Forest Cars
3 Grosvenor Road. Tel: (0342) 325998
Rees Cars
105 Holtye Road. Tel: (0342) 311435
Speedy Taxis
Ashdown Business Centre, 147 London Road. Tel: (0342) 324472

THEATRE
Adeline Genee Theatre
Felcourt Road. Tel: (034 287) 532

᠔ ᠔ ᠔ ᠔ ᠔ ᠔ ᠔

EAST LAVANT

Due north of Chichester, with wonderful views of the downs, East Lavant lies alongside the delightful little Lavant river. An attractive group of cottages huddle around the restored 12th century church.

PUBLIC HOUSE
The Royal Oak
Tel: (0243) 526434

᠔ ᠔ ᠔ ᠔ ᠔ ᠔ ᠔

EAST MARDEN

Along with the other 'Mardens', North, West and Up (but, for some reason, not South) this is among the prettiest, and most remote and unspoilt villages in West Sussex, a true picture-postcard. Flint cottages and farms, and a 12th century church surround a triangular green upon which there is a much-photographed thatched well-head, with a plaque above it reading 'Rest and be Thankful But do not Wreck Me'. Happily, so far no one has.

᠔ ᠔ ᠔ ᠔ ᠔ ᠔ ᠔

EAST PRESTON

A seaside settlement between Littlehampton and Worthing that has a few old cottages near the restored 12th century church, which have been somewhat enveloped by well-manicured and prosperous private housing estates.
Population: 4,702.

HOTELS
Seaview Hotel
127, Sea Road. Tel: (0903) 773988
South Strand Hotel
South Strand. Tel: (0903) 785086
The Three Crowns Hotel
101, Sea Road. BN16 1LS. Tel: (0903) 784074

RESTAURANTS
Bellavista
South Strand. Tel: (0903) 784241
The Old Forge Restaurant
Tel: (0903) 782040
The Village Tandoori Restaurant
130, Sea Road. Tel: (0903) 783398

PUBLIC HOUSES
The Fletcher Arms
Station Road. Tel: (0903) 784858
The Gratwicke Arms
East Street. Tel: (0903) 714041
Roundstone Public House
Roundstone Lane . Tel: (0903) 785423

CAFES & TEA ROOMS
Corner Cafe
Station Road. Tel: (0903) 783403
Polly's Tea Room
109, Sea Road. Tel: (0903) 774983

OTHER AMENITIES
CARAVAN PARK
Roundstone House Caravan Park

EAST MARDEN'S TRIANGULAR GREEN WITH THE THATCHED WELL-HEAD

Roundstone Lane. Tel: (0903) 784444

TAXIS
Be Driven
123, Roundstone Drive. Tel: (0903) 772836
Val's Taxis & Car Hire
20, Lashmar Road. Tel: (0903) 782091

🐦 🐦 🐦 🐦 🐦 🐦 🐦

EAST WITTERING

A popular seaside resort on the Selsey peninsular, merging into its near neighbour, Bracklesham. Holiday camps, caravan parks and seaside bungalows.
Population: 2,532.

HOTELS
Old Barn Hotel & Club
Tamarisk Walk. Tel: (0243) 670928
The Royal Oak Hotel

Stocks Lane. Tel: (0243) 672128
Wittering Lodge Hotel
Shore Road. Tel: (0243) 673207

RESTAURANTS
Boat House Fish & Chip Restaurant
10 Shore Road. Tel: (0243) 673386
Coppers Restaurant
1 The Galleon, Shore Road. Tel: (0243) 672754
Dinks
11 The Parade. Tel: (0243) 671361
Farci's Pizza & Spaghetti House
10 Oakfield Avenue. Tel: (0243) 672990
Jade Garden
38 Shore Road. Tel: (0243) 673220
Parade Parlour
4 The Parade. Tel: (0243) 672172
Raja Indian Restaurant
5 New Parade, Shore Road. Tel: (0243) 673635/672042
Royal Oak Fish Bar
6 Oakfield Road. Tel: (0243) 673309

39

PUBLIC HOUSE

Thatched Tavern
Church Road. Tel: (0243) 673087

CAFES & TEA ROOMS

Boulevard Cafe
40 Shore Road. Tel: (0243) 672617

Galleon Cafe
Shore Road. Tel: (0243) 672422

OTHER AMENITIES

CAR HIRE/SELF DRIVE
Witterings Car Hire
53 Stocks Lane. Tel: (0243) 670004

FLORISTS
Violetta
The Royal Oak, Stocks Lane. Tel: (0243) 673007

LIBRARY
East Wittering Library
Oakfield Avenue. Tel: (0243) 673484

WATER SPORTS
Shore Board Sailing
2 The Galleon, Shore Road. Tel: (0243) 672315

EASTERGATE

A long straggling village, with several new housing estates, north of Bognor Regis. The statue of a lion now acts as a traffic island.
Population: 2,886.

RESTAURANT

Little Chef
A27/A29 Roundabout, Arundel Road. Tel: (0243) 543850

PUBLIC HOUSE

The Wilkes Head
Church Lane. Tel: (0243) 543380

OTHER AMENITIES

CARAVAN PARK
Lidsey Park
Lidsey Road, Lidsey. Tel: (0243) 543265

GARDEN CENTRES
J.D. Godsmark
Grinstead Nurseries, Eastergate Lane. Tel: (0243) 543427

JBS Nurseries
Eastergate Lane. Tel: (0243) 542946

EDBURTON

A tiny village on the spring line beneath a sheer escarpment of the downs. Named after Edburga, King Alfred's grand-daughter, who built a church here in the 10th century. On Edburton Hill stand the prehistoric Castle Rings.

ELMER SANDS

Elmer is at the end of the cul-de-sac that encompasses Middleton-on-Sea. Full of bungalows and holiday camps, it is at its busiest during the summer months. In the storms of 1990 the sea broke over the defences and caused extensive flooding.

HOTELS

Ancton House Hotel
Ancton Lane. Tel: (0243) 582482

Manor Farm Hotel
Ancton Lane. Tel: (0243) 583154

PUBLIC HOUSES

The Cabin Club
Elmer Road. Tel: (0243) 584942

Elmer Hotel
Elmer Road. Tel: (0243) 583520

ELSTED

A compact downland village, close to the Hartings, built from a mixture of brick, flint, tile and thatch. The little rural church has Saxon origins.
Population: 183.

PUBLIC HOUSE

Elsted Inn
Tel: (073 081) 3662

FAYGATE

A small settlement on the edge of the once dense St Leonard's Forest, feared in the Middle Ages for its dragons.

PUBLIC HOUSE

The Holmbush Inn
Faygate Lane. Tel: (029 383) 539

CAFE/TEA ROOMS

Juggernaut Cafe
Horsham Road. Tel: (029 383) 575

FELPHAM

The poet and mystic William Blake, who did something to redress his rakish reputation by writing 'Jerusalem', lived in Felpham. Invited to stay by his friend and mentor William Hayley, whom he later came to loathe, Blake wrote of the village: 'Away to sweet Felpham for heaven is there: The Ladder of Angels descends through the air, On the turret its spiral does softly descend, Through the village it winds, at my cot it does end.' The village is much more populated than in his time, but around Blake's cottage the old flint walls of the winding lanes give the centre of the village a charm that the new estates around and about have failed to match. Limmer Lane was an old smuggling route, and curiously it was wool that was smuggled when it was heavily taxed. Hayley's Corner, a triangular traffic island, is reputed to be haunted. Nearby, The Turret, (of Blake's poem) Hayley's house, has been demolished to make way for flats, highlighting the pressure for building space in this crowded part of Sussex. St Margaret's, in the centre of the village, is a restored Norman church, that contains a monument to William Hayley.

HOTEL
The Beachcroft Hotel & Restaurant
Clyde Road. Tel: (0243) 827142

GUEST HOUSE
Hayleys Corner
14 Limmer Lane. Tel: (0243) 862489
Comfortable Edwardian house in the heart of the village. 2 mins from beach, sailing club, tennis courts, shops, pubs, restaurants.
Months Open: 12. Number of Bedrooms: 5. B&B per person: £14. TV in some rooms. Pets. Evening meals: possibly. Car Park: 6 spaces. Garden. Proprietor: Ms Shirley Moy.

HAYLEYS CORNER GUEST HOUSE

RESTAURANTS
Camelot Restaurant
3 Flansham Lane. Tel: (0243) 585875
Costello's Restaurant
Snooks Corner, 3 Felpham Road. Tel: (0243) 866124
The Cottage Restaurant
58 Felpham Road. Tel: (0243) 863802
The Good Taste Restaurant
Summerley Corner, Summerley Lane. Tel: (0243) 860332
Kam-Too
9 Felpham Road. Tel: (0243) 823375
Ye Olde Malthouse
Waterloo Road. Tel: (0243) 864609
Simla Tandoori
4 Grassmere Parade. Tel: (0243) 822616
Ye Olde Fishe & Chippe Shoppe
78 Felpham Road. Tel: (0243) 822340

PUBLIC HOUSES
Fox Inn
Waterloo Road. Tel: (0243) 865308
The George Inn
102 Felpham Road. Tel: (0243) 824177
Old Barn Free House
Felpham Road. Tel: (0243) 821564
The Southdowns
133 Felpham Way. Tel: (0243) 583916
Thatched House Inn
8 Limmer Lane. Tel: (0243) 865953

CAFES & TEA ROOMS
Boat House Cafe
Blakes Road. Tel: (0243) 826424
Lobster Pot Cafe
Canning Road. Tel: (0243) 862751

OTHER AMENITIES
ART GALLERY
The Felpham Galleries
66 Felpham Road. Tel: (0243) 864044

CAR HIRE/CHAUFFEUR DRIVE
Jojac Car Hire
8 Icarus Way. Tel: (0243) 585333
Stanley Stemp
57 Limmer Lane. Tel: (0243) 821879

CAR HIRE/SELF DRIVE
Milestones Car & Van Rental
Central Garage, 96 Felpham Road. Tel: (0243) 820552

FLORISTS
Floral Fayre
5 Grassmere Parade, Felpham Road. Tel: (0243) 865065

A VIEW FROM BLACKDOWN TOWARDS TELEGRAPH HILL

Jennifer's
6 Summerley Corner, Summerley Lane. Tel: (0243) 863780

LEISURE CENTRE
Arun Leisure Centre
Felpham Way. PO22 8ED Tel: (0243) 826612

🐾 🐾 🐾 🐾 🐾 🐾 🐾

FERNHURST
The last remaining remnant of the Sussex ancient iron-smelting industry is to be found here, close to the Surrey border. Fernhurst is an attractive rural settlement south of Blackdown, set amongst the wooded valleys of the Weald.
Population: 2,780.

🐾 🐾 🐾 🐾 🐾 🐾 🐾

FERRING
Another settlement on the South Coast where holiday housing has swallowed up the original flint village. In Church Lane there are hints of the way things used to be.
Population: 3,896.

HOTEL
Greystoke Manor Hotel
Church Lane. Tel: (0903) 42077

RESTAURANTS
The Capricorn Restaurant
1, Little Paddocks. Tel: (0903) 42454
La Couronne Restaurant
60, Ferring Street. Tel: (0903) 502605
Mohima Tandoori Restaurant
104, Ferring Street. Tel: (0903) 40853
The Pennyfarthing Restaurant
Tel: (0903) 502413
The Rikshaw
Tel: (0903) 770258
Tudor Close
Ferringham Lane. Tel: (0903) 43155/42656

PUBLIC HOUSE
The Henty Arms
Tel: (0903) 41254

CAFE/TEA ROOMS
Lemon Tree Cafe
The Strand. Tel: (0903) 503033

OTHER AMENITIES

CAR HIRE
Cooper Hire
50, Ferring Street . Tel: (0903) 504455

CARAVAN PARKS
Brookline Caravan Park
Brook Lane. Tel: (0903) 42802
Onslow Caravan Park
Onslow Drive. Tel: (0903) 43170
Proprietor: Mr. G.J. Kirby.

GARDEN CENTRES
Country Fayre Market
Old Barn Nursery , Littlehampton Road. Tel: (0903) 45123
The Window Box
33 Church Street, Littlehampton Road. Tel: (0903) 42003

🐾 🐾 🐾 🐾 🐾 🐾 🐾

FINDON
An old village with high flint walls built on a network of lanes, due north of Worthing, that has become connected to the town by means of 'Findon Valley' and is desperately trying to hang on to a separate identity in the face of advancing urbanization. The church, separated from the village by a dual-carriageway is 13th century. The Square in the tiny centre of the village preserves 18th century charm.
Population: 1,528.

HOTELS
Cissbury Hotel
167, Findon Road. Tel: (090 671) 2418
Findon Manor Hotel
High Street. Tel: (090 671) 2733
Village House Hotel
Horsham Road. Tel: (090 671) 3350

GUEST HOUSES
C.W.T. Greenyer
Ramsdean, North End. Tel: (090 671) 2914
Sion Convent
Nepcote Lane. Tel: (090 671) 3171

RESTAURANTS
Darlings Bistro
Tel: (090 671) 3817
The Teahouse
Tel: (090 671) 3365

PUBLIC HOUSES
Black Horse Inn

High Street. Tel: (090 671) 2301
Gun Inn
High Street. Tel: (090 671) 3206
Village House Hotel
The Square, Horsham Road.

OTHER AMENITIES
CAR HIRE
A White Rolls Royce
173, Findon Road. Tel: (090 671) 3493/3838
Bennetts
173, Findon Road. Tel: (090 671) 3838

GARDEN CENTRE
Rogers Farm Garden Centre
Rogers Lane. Tel: (090 671) 3395

ra. ra ra ra ra ra ra

FISHBOURNE
In Roman times Fishbourne, strategically situated on the most northerly inlet of Chichester Harbour, was the port for Chichester, two miles to the east. The advent of the A27 coastal route has effectively cut the community in two, but Fishbourne is now synonymous with the spectacular Roman Palace unearthed twenty odd years ago.

PLACES OF INTEREST
Roman Palace
Tel: (0243) 785859

PUBLIC HOUSE
Black Boy Inn
Main Road. Tel: (0243) 572076

OTHER AMENITY
GARDEN CENTRE
Hangabout
Darringtons, Main Road. Tel: (0243) 572900

ra. ra ra ra ra ra ra

FITTLEWORTH
Situated above the flood plain of the delightful River Rother, in this pleasant village there are some attractive old cottages, a mill house and a very impressive tile-hung inn. Towards the end of his career, Edward Elgar lived in the woods nearby in a thatched cottage called Brinkwells, where he composed many of his works.
Population: 901.

HOTEL
The Swan Hotel
Lower Street. Tel: (079 882) 721

ra. ra ra ra ra ra ra

FIVE OAKS
This little settlement stands on a long straight at the junction of what was Stane Street and the Horsham road. A glance at the map shows how much of the Roman Road survives in this region.

HOTEL
The Five Oaks Inn
Stane Street. Tel: (040 381) 2679

RESTAURANT
The Little Chef
Tel: (040 381) 2711

OTHER AMENITY
CAR HIRE
Billingshurst
Poplar Garage. Tel: (040 381) 4741

ra. ra ra ra ra ra ra

FONTWELL
Dominated by its famous race course, there is no obvious group of buildings.

RESTAURANT
The Fontwell Inn
Arundel Road. Tel: (0243) 543029

OTHER AMENITY
GARDEN CENTRE
Denmans
Denmans Garden Clock House, Denmans. Tel: (0243) 542808

ra. ra ra ra ra ra ra

FORD
As its name suggests, this was the site of a ford across the Arun. St. Andrew's church is one of the prettiest Norman churches in Sussex, but in modern times finds itself to be the next door neighbour of Ford Open Prison, that has boasted many famous inmates, including, recently, poor George Best. There is a continental-style camping site near the river. The wartime airfield is now an industrial estate. There is a market on Sundays.
Population: 367.

GOODWOOD HOUSE, THE SEAT OF THE DUKES OF RICHMOND AND GORDON (SEE OVERLEAF)

PUBLIC HOUSES

The Arundel Arms
Ford Road. Tel: (0903) 882244
Ship & Anchor
Ford Road. Tel: (0243) 551747

OTHER AMENITIES

BOAT MOORINGS
Ship & Anchor Marina
Ford Road. Tel: (0243) 551262

SAUNA
Sussex Tan
E1 Rudford Industrial Estate, Ford Road. Tel: (0903) 730811

🐾 🐾 🐾 🐾 🐾 🐾 🐾

FOXHILL

PUBLIC HOUSE

Fox & Hounds
Tel: (0444) 413242

FULKING

There is a very pleasant walk down from Devil's Dyke to the pub at Fulking below. The walk back uphill is a different matter. This escarpment of the downs is owned by the National Trust, and is riddled with ancient sheep tracks. The ancient hamlet is grouped around a spring at the bottom of the downs.

PUBLIC HOUSE

Shepherd & Dog
The Street. Tel: (079 156) 382

🐾 🐾 🐾 🐾 🐾 🐾 🐾

FUNTINGTON

A small village north-west of Chichester, where the downs meet the plain. The wide main street has some fine Georgian houses.

RESTAURANT

Hallidays of Funtington
Watery Lane. Tel: (0243) 575331

45

PUBLIC HOUSE
Fox & Hounds
Tel: (0243) 575246

🐾 🐾 🐾 🐾 🐾 🐾 🐾

GOODWOOD
Goodwood Racecourse sits right on top of the downs, in the lee of the Trundle, an ancient hill-fort, and the views all around are spectacular. Goodwood is the Estate of the Duke of Richmond, and all the major buildings are part of the Estate. The golf course crosses the road up to the race-course just north of Golf Clubhouse, which used to be the kennels, and is a fine Palladian building. When there are race meetings this area throngs with people, just as it did when Goodwood was also a major motor-racing circuit.

PLACES OF INTEREST
Goodwood House
Tel: (0243) 774107
Built in the 18th century in Sussex flint, Goodwood House is the seat of the Dukes of Richmond and Gordon. The nearby Racecourse, and the now defunct Motor Racing circuit, now the airport, were both part of the Estate. The Queen stays here during Goodwood Week, part of the English summer season. There are fine paintings by Stubbs (of racehorses) and Van Dyck.
Months Open: May-September (closed: event days). Days Open: Sunday & Monday (except in August: Sunday-Thursday). Hours Open: 2-5pm. Bank Holidays: All. Admission: Adult: £2.90, Party: £2.40 (minimum of 20). Children/disabled: £1.70. Superb art collections including paintings by Van Dyck, Canaletto, Reynolds, Romney, Lely. French furniture, Gobelins tapestries, family mementoes including Napoleon's breakfast plate and Queen Victoria's Faberge walking stick - and much more.

HOTEL
Goodwood Park Hotel
Tel: (0243) 775537

OTHER AMENITY
CARAVAN PARK
Goodwood Caravan Park
Tel: (0243) 774486

🐾 🐾 🐾 🐾 🐾 🐾 🐾

GOODWOOD AIRFIELD
The airport sits in the middle of the old motor-racing track, which is still used to test cars. It has been the scene of many triumphs and disasters

over the years; Stirling Moss had a near fatal crash here ending his racing career in 1962, and Bruce McLaren, founder of the hugely successful McLaren team, burnt to death after crashing a test-car here in the late sixties.

RESTAURANT
Goodwood Airfield Restaurant
Tel: (0243) 780117

OTHER AMENITIES
FLYING SCHOOLS
Blades Helicopters
Old Maintenance Building. Tel: (0243) 779222
The GB Air Academy
New Building. Tel: (0243) 531516
Goodwood Flying Club
Tel: (0243) 533813
Goodwood Terrena
The Airfield. Tel: (0243) 774656/781934

🐾 🐾 🐾 🐾 🐾 🐾 🐾

GORING-BY-SEA
Goring lies west of Worthing, indistinguishable from Worthing itself.

GUEST HOUSE
The Court House
Sea lane . Tel: (0903) 48473

RESTAURANTS
Ashalata Tandoori Restaurant
274, Goring Road. Tel: (0903) 501659
The George Toby Grill
39, Goring Road. Tel: (0903) 47226
Rainbows
52, Goring Road. Tel: (0903) 47859
Willow Restaurant
12a, Goring Road . Tel: (0903) 48621

PUBLIC HOUSES
The Bull Inn
Goring Street. Tel: (0903) 48133
Golden Lion
7, Strand.Tel: (0903) 454339
Mulberry Hotel
Goring Road. Tel: (0903) 41555
Sussex Yeoman
Palatine Road. Tel: (0903) 40050

CAFE/TEA ROOMS
Kites
42, Goring Road. Tel: (0903) 504035

OTHER AMENITIES

CAR HIRE

Caffyns
341, Goring Road. Tel: (0903) 504440
Caremore Cars
29, Mersham Gardens. Tel: (0903) 700180
Goring Cars
93, Sea Place. Tel: (0903) 700207
Richacars
Sea Place. Tel: (0903) 700252

🍺 🍺 🍺 🍺 🍺 🍺 🍺

GRAFFHAM

Situated in beautiful countryside south-east of Midhurst, Graffham is a pretty, rural village built on a road that winds its way up to the church, St Giles, below the wooded slopes of the downs. From there is a wonderful view across to the Hogs Back to the north.
Population: 503.

PUBLIC HOUSES

Foresters Arms
Tel: (079 86) 202
White Horse
Tel: (079 86) 331

🍺 🍺 🍺 🍺 🍺 🍺 🍺

HALNAKER

Halnaker Mill is one of the few surviving windmills in this part of the world, and commands a splendid hilltop position. Hilaire Belloc immortalized the mill in one of his poems. The village itself is built along the Chichester-Petworth road. Halnaker House was designed by Lutyens in 1938.

PUBLIC HOUSE

Anglesey Arms
Tel: (0243) 773474

🍺 🍺 🍺 🍺 🍺 🍺 🍺

HAMBROOK

A tiny hamlet in a wooded area north-east of Emsworth in the west of the county.

RESTAURANT

Pieces of Plaice
Hambrook Holiday Camp, Broad Road. Tel: (0243) 572433

OTHER AMENITY

CARAVAN PARK

Hambrook Holiday Camp & Caravan Sites
Broad Road. Tel: (0243) 572658

PUBLIC HOUSE

The Woodmans Arms
Tel: (090 674) 240

🍺 🍺 🍺 🍺 🍺 🍺 🍺

HANDCROSS

A Victorian village lining the road to Brighton, south of Crawley, on the edge of St Leonard's Forest.

PLACES OF INTEREST

Nymans Garden
Tel: (0444) 400321

RESTAURANT

The Red Lion
Tel: (0444) 400292

PUBLIC HOUSES

Fountain Inn
High Street. Tel: (0444) 400218
Easily accessible village pub offering a quality service in a friendly atmosphere. Large parties welcome, preferably by prior arrangement.
Brewery: Whitbread. Licensees: Mr & Mrs Alan Ford. OPEN ALL DAY. Opening Hours: 11.00-11.00. Beer available: Flowers, Strong Country, Whitbread, Best Heineken, Stella, Murphys. Food available: 11.00-9.30pm. Garden. Car Park. Traditional games: Darts, pool, bar billiards.

The Royal Oak (above)
Horsham Road. Tel: (0444) 400703
Typical country pub, family run for 11 years. Egon Ronay Guide for good food - 8 years.
Brewery: Phoenix. Opening Hours: 10.30-3.00, 6.00-11.00. Open all day Fri & Sat. Beer available: Ruddles Best, King & Barnes Festive, Ruddles County, Websters Yorkshire. Food available: 11.30-2.15, 6.15-10.15. Car Park.

47

The Wheatsheaf
Ashfold Crossways, Plummers Plain.Tel: (0444) 400472

CAFE/TEA ROOMS
Sweet Shop & Tea Room
1 Bachelor Buildings , High Street. Tel: (0444) 400259

OTHER AMENITIES
GARDEN CENTRE
Handcross Garden Centre
London Road. Tel: (0444) 400725

TAXI
Handcross Cars
71, West Park Road. Tel: (0444) 400877

🐾 🐾 🐾 🐾 🐾 🐾 🐾

HASSOCKS
A large village immediately north of Brighton, just below the downs.

HOTEL
Hassocks Hotel
Station Approach East. Tel: (079 18) 2113

RESTAURANTS
Friars Oak Toby Grill
Tel: (079 18) 4127
Moonlight Indian Restaurant
5, Keymer Road. Tel: (079 18) 3734

PUBLIC HOUSE
Sandrock Inn
26, High Street .Tel: (0403) 61661

CAFE/TEA ROOMS
Country Style
56, Keymer Road. Tel: (079 18) 3830

OTHER AMENITIES
GARDEN CENTRES
Allwood Bros
Mill Nursery , London Road. Tel: (079 18) 4229
E. G. Budd & Son
South Road. Tel: (079 18) 2412
Eatwoods Nurseries
26, Keymer Road. Tel: (079 18) 4174
Straffords Garden centre
Brighton Road. Tel: (079 18) 5232

TAXI
L.B. Taxi
Station Aproach. Tel: (079 18) 2255

BORDE HILL GARDEN

HAYWARDS HEATH
A town that grew up during the railway age, when both Cuckfield and Lindfield refused to have a railway track bisecting them, so the heathland between the two was used. Many commuters live here, because of the speed of the service to London. St Wilfred's churchyard is said to be the dead centre of Sussex (East and West).

PLACES OF INTEREST
Borde Hill Garden
Tel: (0444) 450326
New lake with picnic area; children's playground; plant sales; dogs on lead; woodland walks; outstanding views; licensed tea rooms and restaurant.
Months Open: End March to End October. Days Open: Monday to Sunday. Hours Open: 10am-6pm. Bank Holidays: Open all Bank Holidays in this period. Admission: £1.50. Children 50p, OAPs £1.00. Particularly beautiful in spring (camellias, rhododendrons, azaleas, magnolias).

HOTEL
Birch Hotel
Lewes Road. Tel: (0444) 45165

GUEST HOUSE
Petit Barbara Bed & Breakfast
61, Franklynn Road. Tel: (0444) 453506

RESTAURANTS
The Beech Hurst Restaurant
Tel: (0444) 412178
The Burger Bun
124, South Road. Tel: (0444) 440530
The Coffee Shop
30, The Orchards. Tel: (0444) 413933
The Curry Inn Tandoori Restaurant
58, Commercial Square. Tel: (0444) 415141
Hilarys
40, The Broadway. Tel: (0444) 458453
Hong Kong Chinese Restaurant

48

8, Commercial Square. Tel: (0444) 412201
Inn The Priory
Tel: (0444) 459533
Modhu Mitha (Tandoori) Restaurant
111, South Road. Tel: (0444) 454661
Nizam Tandoori Restaurant
139, South Road. Tel: (0444) 412794
The Piero's Restaurant
18, Broadway. Tel: (0444) 413580
The Pizza Strada
13, Broadway. Tel: (0444) 413021
The Pops Choice Restaurant
30, Broadway. Tel: (0444) 457144

PUBLIC HOUSES
Fox & Hounds
Fox Hill. Tel: (0444) 413342
The Golden Eagle
American Lane. Tel: (0444) 456826
The Heath
47, Sussex Road.Tel: (0444) 413766
Liverpool Arms Hotel
Clair Road. Tel: (0444) 413710
The Star Inn
Broadway. Tel: (0444) 413267
Sussex Hotel
Sussex Square. Tel: (0444) 454188
Ugly Duckling
27, Wivefield Road.Tel: (0444) 413752

OTHER AMENITIES
ART GALLERY
The Crinan Gallery
95, South Road. Tel: (0444) 417653

BUS & COACH SERVICES
Southdown Motor Services
Gordon Road. Tel: (0444) 451349

CAR HIRE
Acorn Chauffeur Service
3, Orchid Park. Tel: (0444) 450511
Caffyns
Station Garage , Market Place. Tel: (0444) 451511
Parkers Garage
71, Western Road. Tel: (0444) 413672/414355
Suncars
Sandrocks Rocky Lane. Tel: (0444) 456446

GARDEN CENTRE
D. J. Shepherd
23 - 25, Sussex Road. Tel: (0444) 451687

LEISURE CENTRES

WAKEHURST PLACE, ARDINGLY, HAYWARDS HEATH (PAGE 9)

Clair Hall
Perrymount Road. Tel: (0444) 455440
Dolphin Leisure Centre
Pasture Hill Road. Tel: (0444) 457337
Months Open: All year. Days Open: Monday to Sunday. Hours Open: Telephone for details. Bank Holidays: Telephone for details. Swimming, squash, fitness suite, restaurant, bar. Manager: Gill Lake.

STORES
W.H. Smith & Son
65/73, South Road. Tel: (0444) 440032
Woolworths Plc
59, South Road. Tel: (0444) 450508/452634

TAXIS
Census Taxis
Room 6 Frankland Suite , The Priory, Stresham Garden.
Tel: (0444) 440444
Dave's Taxis
10 Winkfield Court, Boltro Road. Tel: (0444) 457600
Haywards Heath Taxis
Taxi Rank. Tel: (0444) 450444
Ranks
Haywards Heath. Tel: (0444) 450444
Selby's Taxis
341, Franklands Village. Tel: (0444) 450001
Station Taxis
Station Aproach. Tel: (0444) 440280

49

HENFIELD

A very pleasant large village, with a bustling main street and some pretty cottages.

Population: 4,345.

HOTELS

The George Hotel
34, High Street. Tel: (0273) 492296

The Plough Inn
High Street. Tel: (0273) 492280

RESTAURANTS

Kents Restaurant
Tel: (0273) 492872

Tottington Manor Hotel & Restaurant
Tel: (0903) 815757

PUBLIC HOUSES

The Bull Inn
London Road, Mockbridge.Tel: (0273) 492232

Cat & Canary
Upper Station Road. Tel: (0273) 492509

Gardeners Arms
Neptown Road. Tel: (0273) 492411

The Raven
High Street. Tel: (0273) 494534

The Wheatsheaf
Woodmancote. Tel: (0273) 492077

White Hart Hotel
High Street. Tel: (0273) 492006

OTHER AMENITIES

BUS & COACH SERVICES
Sussex Bus
Station Road. Tel: (0273) 492611

GARDEN CENTRE
Westlands
West End Lane. Tel: (0273) 492626

TAXI
Henfield Taxi Service
High Street. Tel: (0273) 492571

HEYSHOTT

Situated south of Midhurst in beautiful country-side under the downs, Heyshott is an unpretentious village built around a large village green, where the familiar white-clad cricket players perform their feats in summer.

Population: 331.

HICKSTEAD

Justifiably famous for the International Show-jumping Course situated directly on the main A23, half-way between Crawley and Brighton.

PUBLIC HOUSE

The Castle
London Road. Tel: (044 482) 223

CAFE/TEA ROOMS

Little Chef Restaurant
London Road. Tel: (044 482) 388

HOOKWOOD

A tiny village on the outskirts of Horley, right on the Surrey border, far too close to Gatwick Airport for its own good.

PUBLIC HOUSE

Black Horse Hotel
Reigate Road. Tel: (0293) 782303

OTHER AMENITY

GARDEN CENTRE
Woodside Farm
Reigate Road. Tel: (0293) 785052

HORSHAM

A large country town that battles, like many other places, with too much traffic. The roads are re-routed away from the centre, and pass close to the renowned King & Barnes brewery. There some fine open spaces, including the cricket ground, one of the more charming in the country. The Cause-way, leading to the church, is a secret, hidden part of Horsham with some attractive characteristic buildings, including Horsham Museum. Christ's Hospital, to the south of the town, is in fact a boys' public school, founded originally in the City of London by Edward VI in 1553; it provides much character, with the boys' distinctive 18th century uniform, including bright yellow stockings.

PLACES OF INTEREST

Horsham Museum
9, The Causeway.
Tel: (0403) 54959
Housed in a 16th Century timber-framed building, collections range from Japanese bronzes to 18th Century mouse-traps, from a blacksmith's shop to an unusual flower

garden - in fact, everything from archaeology to zoology. *Months Open: All year round. Days Open: Tuesday to Saturday. Hours Open: 10am-5pm. Admission: Free. As the house is 16th Century and has not been adapted, access for disabled people might be difficult in some cases.*

HOTELS
The Crown Hotel
Carfax. Tel: (0403) 66350
Horsham Wimblehurst Hotel
6, Wimblehurst Road. Tel: (0403) 62319
The Kings Head Hotel
Carfax. Tel: (0403) 53126
Park Hotel & Cafe
7, Park Street. Tel: (0403) 65301

GUEST HOUSES
Alton Guest House
29, Rusper Road. Tel: (0403) 51664
Blatchford House
52, Kings Road. Tel: (0403) 65317
Clarence Guest House
1, Clarence Road. Tel: (0403) 50826
Horsham Beach Guest House
6, Wimblehurst Road. Tel: (0403) 62774

RESTAURANTS
Akash Indian Restaurant
8, Queen Road. Tel: (0403) 64216
Beefeater Restaurant
57, North Street. Tel: (0403) 50141
The Curry Centre
43, London Road. Tel: (0403) 54811
Da-Giovanni Restaurant
19, East Street. Tel: (0403) 55298
Homers Tavern
56, East Street. Tel: (0403) 66761
Hong Kong Chop Suey
25, East Street. Tel: (0403) 64800
Legends Restaurant
3, Denne Road. Tel: (0403) 62029
Merrythought Restaurant
5, Bishopric. Tel: (0403) 54894
Mr Li Chinese Restaurant
47, Springfield Road. Tel: (0403) 50551
Peppers
6a, Market Square. Tel: (0403) 41877
The Pizza Park
16, North Street. Tel: (0403) 50249
Pops Choice Restaurant
25a, Carfax. Tel: (0403) 50513
Raffles Restaurant
Horsham Art Centre, North Street. Tel: (0403) 68689
The River Kwai Restaurant

HORSHAM MUSEUM, HOUSED IN A 16TH CENTURY TIMBER-FRAMED BUILDING

6, Market Square. Tel: (0403) 62122
Shahi Tandoori Restaurant
66, East Street. Tel: (0403) 50348
St. Peters Cottage Restaurant
Tel: (0403) 864324
Wimpy Restaurant
39b, West Street. Tel: (0403) 60625

PUBLIC HOUSES
The Anchor Inn
East Street.
The Bell Inn
Park Street. Tel: (0403) 53756
Boars Head Tavern & Restaurant
Worthing Road. RH13 7AD Tel: (0403) 54353
Coot Inn
Merryfield Drive. Tel: (0403) 65744
The Dog & Bacon
North Parade. Tel: (0403) 52176
The Dun Horse Inn
Brighton Road, Mannings Heath. Tel: (0403) 65783
Forresters Arms
43 St. Leonard Road. Tel: (0403) 54458
The Fountain Inn
81, Rusper Road. Tel: (0403) 55428
Green Dragon
12, Bishopric. Tel: (0403) 65047

The Hop Picker
North Parade. Tel: (0403) 64927
Hornbrook Inn
Brighton Road, Hornbrook Hill.Tel: (0403) 52638
Hurst Arms
31, North Street.Tel: (0403) 53526
Kings Arms
Bishopric. Tel: (0403) 53588
Michell Arms
Springfield Road. Tel: (0403) 54543
Queens Head
Queen Street. Tel: (0403) 52721
The Rising Sun
Pondtail Road. Tel: (0403) 53463
St. Leonards Arms
51, Brighton Road.Tel: (0403) 720010
Stout House
Carfax. Tel: (0403) 67777
The Tanners Arms
78, Brighton Road.Tel: (0403) 50527

CAFES & TEA ROOMS

Cavalier Cafe
15, Bishopric. Tel: (0403) 54059
Jups Cafe
9, Brighton Road. Tel: (0403) 60445
Pepe's Snack Bar
16, Fitzalan Road. Tel: (0403) 66116

OTHER AMENITIES
ART GALLERIES
The Gentle Gallery
2 Shelley House , The Bishopric. Tel: (0403) 58567
Horsham Arts Centre
North Steet. Tel: (0403) 68689

CAR HIRE
Caffyns
Springfield Road. Tel: (0403) 54311
Hurst Autos
4, Roffeyhurst Forest Road. Tel: (0403) 65487
Lockyear Motors
Plummers Plain. Tel: (0403) 76466
Tanfield Garage
Guildford Road . Tel: (0403) 61393

CINEMA
Horsham Arts Centre-Ritz Cinema
North Street. Tel: (0403) 68689

GARDEN CENTRE
The Hillier Garden Centre
Hornbrook Nursery, Brighton Road. Tel: (0403) 210113/
210107

HEALTH CLUBS
Body Shop
5, Middle Street. Tel: (0403) 59172
Horsham Diet Centre
7a, Queen Street. Tel: (0403) 211740
Tip Top Health Club
49a, East Street. Tel: (0403) 56369

NIGHT CLUB
Champagne Night Club
Court Royal Theatre, Carfax. Tel: (0403) 66294

SNOOKER CENTRE
Green Baize Billiards & Snooker Centre
77, Rusper Road. Tel: (0403) 50147

STORES
Chart & Lawrence
8, Carfax. Tel: (0403) 64091
Marks & Spencer plc
2, Swan Walk. Tel: (0403) 59355

TAXIS
Apollo Taxis
75a, Park Terrace East. Tel: (0403) 51777
Atlas Taxis
56, North Street. Tel: (0403) 52888
Burman's Taxi Service
Salisbury Road. Tel: (0403) 52792
Fairways Taxis
Tel: (0403) 51414
Montana Taxis
Tel: (0403) 69044

THEATRE
Capitol Theatre
Norh Street. Tel: (0403) 68689

ഇ ഇ ഇ ഇ ഇ ഇ ഇ

HOUGHTON

Pronounced 'hoe-ton' by indigenous locals, there is one long downhill street, leading to a causeway and the bridge across the Arun, and Amberley. The George and Dragon enjoys splendid views of part of the South Downs Way from its garden, and claims to have entertained Charles II when he was fleeing the Roundheads.(See Amberley.)
Population: 88.

PUBLIC HOUSES
Bridge Inn
Tel: (0798) 831619

52

HOUSES IN HORSHAM

George & Dragon
Tel: (0798) 831559

CAFE/TEA ROOMS
Houghton Bridge Riverside Tea Rooms & Gardens
Tel: (0798) 831558

🍃 🍃 🍃 🍃 🍃 🍃 🍃

HUNSTON
A small village immediately south of Chichester, stretched along the main road to Selsey. There is a popular local pub.
Population: 1,121.

PUBLIC HOUSE
The Spotted Cow
Tel: (0243) 786718

OTHER AMENITIES
TAXIS
Blue Line Taxis

18 High Bank. Tel: (0243) 774279/774077
P.J.S. (Hiring)
64 St. Leodegars Way. Tel: (0243) 774389

🍃 🍃 🍃 🍃 🍃 🍃 🍃

HURSTPIERPOINT
A pleasant village south-west of Burgess Hill. There is a Victorian church with a tall tower that rises above some fine Georgian houses in the High Street. One mile to the north is the public school, Hurstpierpoint, founded by the same cleric who founded Lancing and Ardingly, the Rev. Nathanial Woodard.
Population: 5,543.

RESTAURANTS
Memories of India
122, High St. Tel: (0273) 833156
Sears Restaurant
117, High Street. Tel: (0273) 833452
Daniels Restaurant
120, High Street. Tel: (0273) 832183

53

PUBLIC HOUSES

Duke Of York Inn
London Road. Tel: (0273) 832262
The New Inn
76, High Street.Tel: (0273) 834608
The Pierpoint
71, Western Road.Tel: (0273) 832241
The Poacher
139, High Street.Tel: (0273) 834893
The White Horse Inn
High Street. Tel: (0273) 834717

OTHER AMENITIES

NIGHT CLUB
Spencers
Sayers Common. Tel: (0273) 833232

TAXI
Hurst Taxis
10, Nursery Close. Tel: (0273) 833934

🐾 🐾 🐾 🐾 🐾 🐾 🐾

IFIELD

An old settlement that now forms part of Crawley, Ifield is on the western outskirts of the New Town, with views across farmland from the churchyard of the 13th century St. Margaret's. There is a vestige of the old village, with some old cottages and an attractive pub.

HOTELS
Brooklyn Manor
Bonnetts Lane. Tel: (0293) 546024
Ifield Court Hotel
Charlwood Road. Tel: (0293) 34807

GUEST HOUSE
Caprice Guest House
Bonnets Lane. Tel: (0293) 28620

PUBLIC HOUSES
Gate Inn
Rusper Road. Tel: (029 384) 271
The Plough Inn
Ifield Street. Tel: (0293) 24292
The Royal Oak
Ifield Green. Tel: (0293) 26959

GUEST HOUSE
Prestwood House Guest House
Prestwood House , Prestwood Lane. Tel: (0293) 20055

🐾 🐾 🐾 🐾 🐾 🐾 🐾

ITCHENOR

A sailing village on Chichester Harbour, on a no-through road with a shingle foreshore at the end. There is an old ferry across to Bosham, and there are some very pleasant private houses lining the main street, and a pub and a 13th century church half a mile from the harbour.

HOTEL
The Ship Inn
The Street. Tel: (0243) 512284

🐾 🐾 🐾 🐾 🐾 🐾 🐾

KEYMER

The village has now joined up with Hassocks to create a sizeable settlement. The church is dedicated, unusually, to St. Cosmas and St. Damian, and has Norman origins. There is an 18th century windmill.
Population: 5,372.

PUBLIC HOUSES
Greyhound Inn
Keymer Road. Tel: (079 18) 2645
The Thatched Inn
Grand Avenue . Tel: (079 18) 2946

🐾 🐾 🐾 🐾 🐾 🐾 🐾

KINGSFOLD

A village very close to the Surrey border, north of Horsham.

PUBLIC HOUSE
The Dog & Duck
Dorking Road. Tel: (030 679) 295

🐾 🐾 🐾 🐾 🐾 🐾 🐾

KIRDFORD

There are still some huge oak trees, remnants of the ancient forests that covered the Weald, around Kirdford, an old glass-making centre. A row of horse-chestnut trees dominate the centre of the village, around a tiny green. Below the town sign is a potted history of Kirdford.
Population: 927.

PUBLIC HOUSES
Forrester Arms
Tel: (040 377) 205
The Half Moon

LANCING COLLEGE, SET AGAINST THE DOWNS, AND ITS IMPOSING CHAPEL ARE VISIBLE FROM THE MAIN A27

LAGNESS

A very small community, manifest mainly in the Royal Oak public house, between Pagham and Chichester.

PUBLIC HOUSE
Royal Oak
Tel: (0243) 262216

🐚 🐚 🐚 🐚 🐚 🐚 🐚

LANCING

Lancing College is a famous boys' public school (see Hurstpierpoint), and both the school and the imposing chapel are visible from the main A27, set against the downs. The road now by-passes the village, leaving some buildings of character. Pre-war bungalows stretch down to the sea, but happily post-war planning has prevented the construction of more.
Population: 17,073.

HOTEL
Sussex Pad Hotel
Old Shoreham Road. Tel: (0273) 454647
Once the haunt of smugglers, now the haunt of lovers of fine food and wines.
BEDROOMS: 6 Double, (6 en suite,) B&B £ 52.00. 3 Twin, (3 en suite,) B&B £ 52.00. 1 Family, (1 en suite,) £ 52.00. RESTAURANT: English/French Cuisine. Lunch: £ 17.00. Dinner: £ 17.00. House Wine: £ 7.40. À La Carte: £ 17.00. Specialities: fish. HOTEL INFORMATION: CF. W. B. F. 100 space Car Park. Dogs. Credit Cards: Ac. Recommendations: AA. ER.
Weekend Breaks: 2 nights: £ 60.00. 3 nights: £ 75.00.

GUEST HOUSES
Beach Guest House
81, Brighton Road. Tel: (0903) 753368
Moorings Guest House
71, Brighton Road. Tel: (0903) 755944
Seaways Guest House
83, Brighton Road. Tel: (0903) 752338

55

Shoresand House
73, Brighton Road. Tel: (0903) 764537

RESTAURANTS
Almarina Tandoori Restaurant
2, Western Road. Tel: (0903) 752647
Casa de Napoli
34, South Street. Tel: (0903) 764828
The Minstrels Gallery
Tel: (0903) 766777
The Odd Spot Restaurant
170, South Street. Tel: (0903) 754886
Robins Nest Restaurant
132, South Street. Tel: (0903) 752687
Shoestrings
140, South Street. Tel: (0903) 750702
The Sussex Potter
43, Manor Road. Tel: (0903) 733210

PUBLIC HOUSES
Farmers Hotel
17, South Street.Tel: (0903) 753097
The Merry Monk
1, North Road.Tel: (0903) 753316
Three Horseshoes Inn
182, South Street.Tel: (0903) 753424

CAFES & TEA ROOMS
The Coffee Shop
18, North Road. Tel: (0903) 755959
The Eatwell
3, Queens Way. Tel: (0903) 765789
Mermaid Cafeteria
28a, Brighton Road. Tel: (0903) 753024
The Picnic
3, South Street. Tel: (0903) 767831

OTHER AMENITIES
CAR HIRE
Airport Cars
111, Kings Road. Tel: (0903) 755734/761333 (fax)
Airport, seaport, long distance car hire
Months Open: All year. Days Open: 7 days per week. Hours
Open: 8am-8pm office. 24 hour service. Bank Holidays: open.
Specialist taxi service to airports, seaports and long distance
journeys only. Cars to carry 1-8 passengers and luggage. Same
price day or night. Accept Visa and Access cards. Reliable service
both to and from all major airports/seaports. No fuss. No worry.
Rates: Please call for price quotes. Proprietor: Mr IR Taylor.
Coopers
215, Brighton Road. Tel: (0903) 762599
F.B. Motors Hire
12, Spencer Road. Tel: (0903) 763611

Sussex Carriage Company
41, South Street. Tel: (0903) 767784

CARAVAN PARKS
A.S. Jenkinson
Golden Sands Caravan Park, Brighton Road. Tel: (0903) 752701
Happy Days Caravan Site
10, Old Salt Farm Road. Tel: (0903) 752755

LEISURE CENTRE
Lancing Manor Leisure Centre
Old Shoreham Road. Tel: (0903) 764219

NIGHT CLUB
Keystones
140, South Street. Tel: (0903) 755121

STORE
Woolworths
25, North Road. Tel: (0903) 753963

TAXIS
Access cars
Station Forecourt , South Street. Tel: (0903) 755533
Atomic Cars
1a, Station Parade. Tel: (0903) 752541
Broadway Cars Taxi Service
425, Brighton Road. Tel: (0903) 763522
Lancing Radio Taxis
Station Forecourt, South Street. Tel: (0903) 753607
Ranks
Lancing Station. Tel: (0903) 753607
Shoreham Airport
Brighton Road. Tel: (0903) 766121
Sompting Car Hire
Tel: (0903) 753165

 za za za za za za za

LAVANT
Lavant is a group of small villages, East,West and Mid Lavant, north of Chichester, just below the downs. They manage to retain a rural charm, although so close to the city.
Population: 1,437.

HOTEL
The Hunters Lodge Hotel
Midhurst Road. Tel: (0243) 527329

PUBLIC HOUSE
The Earl of March
Lavant Road. Tel: (0243) 774751

LICKFOLD

A hamlet in the beautiful wooded countryside south of Blackdown with a wonderful collection of 16th and 17th century timber-framed cottages.

PUBLIC HOUSE

The Lickfold Inn

Tel: (079 85) 285

🐚 🐚 🐚 🐚 🐚 🐚 🐚

LINDFIELD

In spite of now being almost part of Haywards Heath, Lindfield manages to retain a separate identity, and has a fine half-mile High Street leading up to the church. The wide common was used for fairs and markets in medieval times, and the combination of brick and tile-hung houses, some of them colour-washed, make this village one of the most picturesque in the county. St John the Baptist is a mainly 13th and 14th century church. Its tall spire was a landmark for miles around when the area was heavily forested.

HOTEL

The Bent Arms Hotel

98 High Street. Tel: (044 47) 3146

RESTAURANT

Araminta Authentic Tandoori Restaurant

107, High Street. Tel: (044 47) 3124

PUBLIC HOUSES

The Linden Tree

47, High Street.Tel: (044 47) 2995

The Snowdrop Inn

Snowdrop Lane. Tel: (0444) 412487

The White Horse

The Pond High Street. Tel: (044 47) 2251

OTHER AMENITIES

TAXIS

P.G. Anderson

79, Newton Road. Tel: (044 47) 4525

Newnhams Taxis

107, The Welkin. Tel: (044 47) 3491

🐚 🐚 🐚 🐚 🐚 🐚 🐚

LITTLEHAMPTON

Along with its near neighbour, Bognor Regis, Littlehampton is often the butt of music-hall jokes, largely because of its name. Situated at the mouth of the River Arun, the original town is on the east bank, consisting of flint cottages. When the fever for seaside resorts hit in the early 19th century, new terraces were built further to the east, almost creating two towns. It was in Littlehampton that the Body Shop empire was created, and their international headquarters are still in the town. *Population: 21,974.*

HOTELS

The Arun View Inn

Wharf Road. Tel: (0903) 722335

The Beach Hotel

22 South Terrace. Tel: (0903) 717277

Colbern Hotel

71, South Terrace. Tel: (0903) 714270

BEDROOMS: 2 Single, (2 TV, 2 tea/coffee) B&B £ 17.50 - £ 20.00. 3 Double, (3 en suite, 3 TV, 3 tea/coffee) B&B £ 17.50 - £ 20.00. 3 Twin, (3 en suite, 3 TV, 3 tea/coffee) B&B £ 17.50 - £ 20.00. 1 Family, (1 en suite, 1 TV, 1 tea/coffee) £ 17.50 - £ 20.00. RESTAURANT: English Cuisine. Dinner: £ 7.50. Sports Facilities: Golf . Riding . Fishing. Tennis. Swimming pool,Bowls, squash all nearby. . Credit Cards: Ac. Am. D. V. Weekend Breaks: 2 nights: £ 35.00. 3 nights: £ 52.50.

The Crown Hotel

29, High Street. Tel: (0903) 713318

Fairview Private Hotel

93, South Terrace. Tel: (0903) 726095

Marine Hotel

Selbourne Road. Tel: (0903) 721476

The New Inn

Norfolk Road. Tel: (0903) 713112

Regency Hotel

85, South Terrace. Tel: (0903) 717707

On sea front opposite greens.

BEDROOMS: 1 Single, (1 en suite, 1 TV, 1 tea/coffee) B&B £ 18.00 - £ 20.00. 4 Double, (4 en suite, 4 TV, 4 tea/coffee) B&B £ 32.00 - £ 38.00. 1 Twin, (1 en suite, 1 TV, 1 tea/coffee) B&B £ 32.00 - £ 38.00. 2 Family, (2 en suite, 2 TV, 2 tea/coffee) £ 40.00 - £ 50.00. Credit Cards: Ac.

GUEST HOUSES

Banjo Guest House

4, Fitzalan Road. Tel: (0903) 725338

Beachside Guest House

61, Beach Head Road. Tel: (0903) 715782

Homelight Guest House

43, Bayford Road. Tel: (0903) 713611

Off-Shore

4, St Augustine road. Tel: (0903) 715026

Sharoleen Guest House

85, Bayfords Road. Tel: (0903) 713464

Southwood Guest House

42, Arundel Road. Tel: (0903) 714451

Sunnyvale Guest House
64, Arundel road. Tel: (0903) 714265
Victoria Private Hotel
New Road. Tel: (0903) 717175

RESTAURANTS
Balaton Restaurant
51, Pier Road. Tel: (0903) 713113
Bassil's
8 / 10, Arcade Road. Tel: (0903) 722055
Beggars Roost
Tel: (0903) 714077
Chopstick
2, Beach Road. Tel: (0903) 715696
The Ferry Cafe
46, Pier Road. Tel: (0903) 723766
Mortimers
9, Norfolk Road. Tel: (0903) 713670
The Rice Bowl
129, East Street. Tel: (0903) 714036
The River Breeze
57, Pier Road. Tel: (0903) 722330
The Riverside Restaurant
Tel: (0903) 715966
Royal Restaurant
59, Pier Road. Tel: (0903) 716888
Seahorse Floating Restaurant
Tel: (0903) 724916
The Sussex House
11, High Street. Tel: (0903) 716566
Vardar Restaurant
3, Selbourne Place. Tel: (0903) 721226

PUBLIC HOUSES
Britannia Inn
Pier Road. Tel: (0903) 713235
The Globe Inn
Duke Street. Tel: (0903) 716557
The Locomotive
74, Lyminster Road.Tel: (0903) 716658
Nelson Hotel
61, Pier Road.Tel: (0903) 713358
The Spotted Cow
5 - 7, East Street.Tel: (0903) 713189
Steam Packet
54, River Road.Tel: (0903) 715994
White Hart Inn
Surrey Street. Tel: (0903) 713324
Wickbourne Swan
Clun Road. Tel: (0903) 713680

CAFES & TEA ROOMS
Brennies Cafe
1, Queen Street. Tel: (0903) 715869

The Coffee Cub
15c, Surrey Street. Tel: (0903) 725214
Copperfields
37, Surrey Street. Tel: (0903) 715119
Crumbs Cafe
22, High Street. Tel: (0903) 713726
The Harbour View
29, Pier Road. Tel: (0903) 717918
Jason's Cafe
22, High Street. Tel: (0903) 713726
Leeside
Rope Walk. Tel: (0903) 723666
Marine Cafe
Marina Rope Walk. Tel: (0903) 722154
Norfolk Gardens Cafe
Norfolk Gardens. Tel: (0903) 725326
Roma Cafe
6, Terminus Road. Tel: (0903) 726401
Seagull Cafe
45, Pier Road. Tel: (0903) 715790
Sergeant Peppers
3 / 4, Terminus Road. Tel: (0903) 717450
South Farm Cafe
16, South Farm Road. Tel: (0903) 715729
Wimpy Restaurant
8, Surrey Street. Tel: (0903) 722213

OTHER AMENITIES
CAR HIRE
A. C. Car Hire
St. Martins Barn, Arundel Road. Tel: (0903) 713625
Swan Line 84
31b, High Street. Tel: (0903) 723937

CAR HIRE/SELF DRIVE
Mida
4 Terminus Road. Tel: (0903) 717271

CARAVAN PARK
Weir Associates
73, High Street . Tel: (0903) 726262

GARDEN CENTRES
Mill Lane Nursery
Mill Lane Wick. Tel: (0903) 716972
Ockendens
Garden Centre , St. Martins Lane. Tel: (0903) 713046

HEALTH CLUB
Dimension Health & Fitness Centre
2, Beach Road. Tel: (0903) 713063
The Canadian village
Rope Walk. Tel: (0903) 713816

SNOOKER CENTRE
Tower Snooker Club
8 - 10 Clifton Road . Tel: (0903) 726320

STORE
Woolworths
19, Surrey Street. Tel: (0903) 713646

TAXIS
Arun Taxis
1 Bayford Road. Tel: (0903) 717832
Garys Taxis
Station Aproach. Tel: (0903) 726666

🐾 🐾 🐾 🐾 🐾 🐾 🐾

LITTLEWORTH

PUBLIC HOUSE
Windmill Inn
Littleworth Lane. Tel: (0403) 710308

🐾 🐾 🐾 🐾 🐾 🐾 🐾

LODSWORTH

Situated in beautiful countryside between Petworth and Midhurst, a pretty village with a main
street winding among a pleasant mixture of old
and new buildings.
Population: 650.

PUBLIC HOUSES
Halfway Bridge
Tel: (079 85) 281
Hollist Arms
The Street. Tel: (079 85) 471 /310

OTHER AMENITY
ART GALLERY
Jeremy Wood Fine Art
19/21 East Street. Tel: (0798) 43408

🐾 🐾 🐾 🐾 🐾 🐾 🐾

LOWER BEEDING

For some typically British reason, Lower Beeding
is over ten miles NORTH of Upper Beeding. (It has
been suggested that in fact their names refer to
their importance, rather than geography. And there
are other much more involved explanations.) Standing on the edge of St Leonards Forest, south of
Horsham, the village is somewhat scattered around
a road junction.
Population: 3,034.

PLACES OF INTEREST
Leonardslee Gardens
Extensive spring-flowering valley garden with rhododen-
drons and azaleas, fabulous trees, lakes, rock garden,
wallabies, deer parks. 3 miles from M23 via Handcross
(A279).
*Months Open: April to October. Days Open: Monday to
Sunday April to June; weekends only June to October. Hours
Open: 10-6pm April to June; 12-6pm June to September; 10-5pm
Oct. Admission: Varies with season. Licensed restaurant; cafe;
plants and souvenirs for sale..*

HOTELS
Brookfield Farm Hotel
Winter Pit Lane. Tel: (040 376) 568
South Lodge Hotel
Brighton Road. Tel: (040 376) 711

PUBLIC HOUSES
The Crabtree
A281. Tel: (0403) 891257
The Plough
Leechpong Hill. Tel: (040 376) 277

OTHER AMENITY
GARDEN CENTRE
Howards Nursery Centre
Handcross Road, Plummers Plain. Tel: (040 376) 255

🐾 🐾 🐾 🐾 🐾 🐾 🐾

LOWFIELD HEATH

A village whose destiny has been shaped by its
proximity to Gatwick Airport. Administratively in
Surrey, but in fact a parish of Crawley.

HOTELS
The Gatwick Concorde Hotel
Church Road. Tel: (0293) 33441
The Gatwick Grove Guest House
Poles Lane. Tel: (0293) 515795
Gatwick Manor Inn
London Road. Tel: (0293) 26301

PUBLIC HOUSE
The Flight Tavern
Charlwood Road. Tel: (0293) 552596

OTHER AMENITY
CAR HIRE
Brititish Car Rental
Concorde Hotel, Church Road. Tel: (0293) 551881

🐾 🐾 🐾 🐾 🐾 🐾 🐾

THE RECTORY AT LURGASHALL

LOXWOOD

Close to the Surrey border west of Horsham, pleasant cottages, a duck pond and a row of shops make up this little village.
Population: 1,328.

PUBLIC HOUSES
The Onslow Arms
High Street. Tel: (0403) 752452
The Sir Roger Tichborn
Tel: (0403) 752377

🍺 🍺 🍺 🍺 🍺 🍺 🍺

LURGASHALL

A beautiful village north-west of Petworth with stone and tile-hung houses surrounding a triangular village green, with a cricket square in the middle. The archetypal English village, with pub and church in close proximity to one another in one corner of the green.
Population: 576.

PUBLIC HOUSE
Noahs Ark
Tel: (0428) 78346

🍺 🍺 🍺 🍺 🍺 🍺 🍺

LYMINSTER

Lyminster has become somewhat absorbed by Littlehampton to the south. It is in fact an ancient settlement, the site of a 10th century Benedictine nunnery. There is a 13th century church, and some houses and walls are made of flint.
Population: 303.

AMENITY
CARAVAN PARKS
Brookside Holiday Camp
Lyminster Road. Tel: (0903) 713292

🍺 🍺 🍺 🍺 🍺 🍺 🍺

MAPLEHURST

A remote village in the thickly-wooded Weald, south of Horsham, with some old houses, and tile-and-weatherboard barns.

PUBLIC HOUSE
The White Horse Inn
Park Lane. Tel: (040 376) 208

🍺 🍺 🍺 🍺 🍺 🍺 🍺

MERSTON

A surprisingly remote and rural little village, although only a couple of miles from Chichester. St Giles, a 13th century church, is delightfully situated among tall trees.

PUBLIC HOUSE
The Kings Head
Bognor Road. Tel: (0243) 783576

OTHER AMENITY
GARDEN CENTRE
Country Gardens at Chichester
Fiveacres Nurseries, Bognor Road. Tel: (0243) 789276/781319

🍺 🍺 🍺 🍺 🍺 🍺 🍺

MIDDLETON-ON-SEA

A largely residential area to the east of Bognor, that has some splendid and expensive homes around Sea Lane, the old road down to the sea. The property gets cheaper eastwards towards Elmer, and much less interesting. There is restricted access to the beach in Middleton, there are many 'private' estates, although there are still one or two fields left among the houses. At one time the village was two miles inland, and there is a sunken village due south of Middleton, in the English Channel.
Population: 2,946.

RESTAURANT
Bow Window
Middleton Road. Tel: (0243) 582232

THE SPREAD EAGLE BEYOND THE DUCK POND AT MIDHURST

PUBLIC HOUSE
The Beresford Hotel
Elmer Road. Tel: (0243) 585023/582049/585023

OTHER AMENITIES
CAR HIRE/CHAUFFEUR DRIVE
E.G. Beach
12 Lodge Close. Tel: (0243) 583006

HOLIDAY CAMP
Sussex Coast
10 Main Drive. Tel: (0243) 582221

SAUNA
Sussex Tan
8 Guernsey Farm Lane. Tel: (0243) 694691/584691

TAXI
Red Cab
4 Lucking Lane. Tel: (0243) 585540

MIDHURST
A beautiful country town, with some fine old buildings, and twisting, turning lanes. In Red Lion Square stands the old timbered market house, just

beyond the splendid 15th century coaching inn, the Spread Eagle. The oddly-named Knockhundred Row curves round into the wide main street, North Street, which has some fine Georgian houses and the elegant Angel Hotel. The Estate is owned by the Cowdray family, who have done much to retain Midhurst's charm, and their distinctive yellow painted cottages are scattered throughout the town and surrounding countryside. This is a beautiful part of Sussex, the whole area is a visual delight, and the atmosphere is of relaxed gentility. The ruins of Cowdray House lie to the north of the town, and Cowdray Park is one of the country's major polo centres.
Population: 4,020.

PLACES OF INTEREST
Cowdray Park
The ruins of the 'cursed' house, destroyed by fire in 1793, the seat of the Earls of Southampton. Polo is played in the superb parkland.

HOTELS
The Angel Hotel
North Street. Tel: (073 081) 2421/3253
The Spread Eagle Hotel
South Street. Tel: (073 081) 6911

THE RUINS OF THE CURSED COWDRAY HOUSE

RESTAURANTS

Asha Tandoori Restaurant
Rumbolds Hill. Tel: (073 081) 4113
The Coffee Pot
Knockhundred Market, Knockhundred Row. GU29 9DQ
Tel: (0730) 815113
Good-Year
3 North Street. Tel: (073 081) 3700
Hindle Wakes Restaurant
1 Church Hill. Tel: (073 081) 3371
Maxine's Restaurant
Elisabeth House, Red Lion Street. Tel: (073 081) 6271
The Mida Restaurant
Rumbolds Hill. Tel: (073 081) 3284
Mughal Tandoori Restaurant
135 North Street. Tel: (073 081) 2998
Old Manor House Restaurant
Church Hill. Tel: (073 081) 2990
Squires Wine Bar & Restaurant
Rumbolds Hill. Tel: (073 081) 2544
The Tasty Plaice

Rumbolds Hill. Tel: (073 081) 4753

PUBLIC HOUSES

The Bricklayers Arms
Wool Lane. Tel: (073 081) 2084
The Crown Inn
Edinburgh Square. Tel: (073 081) 3462
Traditional 16th century pub with open fires. Monthly spit roast lamb. Home-made food always available. Function room to rear.
Brewery: Phoenix. Licensee: Mr Paul Stevens. OPEN ALL DAY. Opening Hours: 11.00-11.00. Beer available: Ruddles Best & County, Websters Yorkshire, Gale HSB. Food available: At all times. 3 Bedrooms: B&B per person: £ 12.50. Traditional games: Darts, pool, dominoes, board games.
The Egmont Arms
Rumbolds Hill. Tel: (073 081) 3050
The Greyhound
Cocking Causeway. Tel: (073 081) 3300
Half Moon Inn
Petersfield Road. Tel: (073 081) 2717

The Richard Cobden Inn
Tel: (073 081) 2974

The Swan Inn
Red Lion Street. Tel: (0730) 812853
15th century low beamed bar and restaurant. Victorian public bar. Cosy atmosphere, children welcome. *Brewery: Harvey & Son (Lewes) Ltd. OPEN ALL DAY. Beer available: Harveys Best Bitter, Armada Ale, Harveys Pale Ale, Carling Lager, Holsten Lager. Food available: Noon - 9.30pm. 3 Bedrooms: B&B per person: £ 25.00. Car park. Traditional games: Darts and quiz games.*

Three Horseshoes
North Street. Tel: (073 081) 5580

The Wheatsheaf
Wool Lane. Tel: (073 081) 3450

THE SWAN INN, MIDHURST

CAFE/TEA ROOMS
The Crusty Loaf
North Street. Tel: (073 081) 3892

OTHER AMENITIES
CARAVAN PARK
Holmbush Caravan Park
Bourne Way. Tel: (073 081) 3288

FLORISTS
The Posy Bowl
Knockhundred Market, Knockhundred Row. Tel: (073 081) 2077

LEISURE CENTRE
The Grange Centre
Bepton Road. Tel: (0730) 816841

LIBRARY
Midhurst Library
Midhurst Street, Knockhundred Row. Tel: (073 081) 3564

TAXIS
Easebourne Taxis
3 The Mint Market, Grange Road. Tel: (073 081) 6895

Joyce's Car Hire
5 St. Richards Flat, June Lane. Tel: (073 081) 4292

White's Car Hire
5 Sandrock, June Lane. Tel: (073 081) 3382

🐦 🐦 🐦 🐦 🐦 🐦 🐦

NORTH BERSTED
One of the original villages that now make up Bognor Regis, North Bersted is now indistinguishable from the rest of the town. One or two thatched cottages are scattered among an otherwise unremarkable suburb.

PUBLIC HOUSE
Royal Oak
336 Chichester Road. Tel: (0243) 869018/821002

OTHER AMENITIES
CARAVAN PARK
Orchard Caravan Park
Chichester Road. Tel: (0243) 864063

TAXI
Ace Taxis
11a Royal Parade. Tel: (0243) 865711

🐦 🐦 🐦 🐦 🐦 🐦 🐦

NORTH HEATH
A tiny settlement situated on the long straight between Pulborough and Billingshurst, on what was Stane Street.

CAFE/TEA ROOMS
Toat Cafe
Stane Street. Tel: (079 82) 2113

🐦 🐦 🐦 🐦 🐦 🐦 🐦

NORTH MUNDHAM
Paired with South Mundham, this is a straggling village set in cornfields at the top of the Selsey peninsular.
Population: 1,141.

OTHER AMENITY
GARDEN CENTRE
Southgate Nursery
Fisher Lane. Tel: (0243) 783685

🐦 🐦 🐦 🐦 🐦 🐦 🐦

63

NORTHGATE

A parish now absorbed by the New Town of Crawley.

PUBLIC HOUSE

Black Dog
Barnfield Road. Tel: (0293) 26628

🍺 🍺 🍺 🍺 🍺 🍺 🍺

NUTBOURNE

On the railway line between Emsworth and Chichester there is a succession of 'bournes; Southbourne, Nutbourne, and Fishbourne. Nutbourne is part of the ribbon development along the main A27, but some tiny lanes do run to the south down to Chichester Harbour. Blends into its near neighbour, Southbourne.

RESTAURANTS

The Cedar Tree Restaurant
Main Road. Tel: (0243) 573149
Little Chef
Main Road. Tel: (0243) 373683

PUBLIC HOUSES

The Barley Mow
Main Road. Tel: (0243) 573172
The Bell & Anchor
Main Road. Tel: (0243) 372743
Victorian building with large car park and large garden with children's play area. Snacks available lunchtimes. *Brewery: Friary Meux/Ind Coope. Licensee: Mr AJ Arnell. Opening Hours: 11am-2.30pm, 6pm-11pm. Beer available: 2 real ales, 2 lagers, mild, 2 keg bitters, cider. Food available: lunchtime. 4 Bedrooms: B&B per person: £12.50. Garden. Large car park. Traditional games: Darts, cribbage.*

OTHER AMENITY

GARDEN CENTRE
Nutbourne Nurseries
Stream Lane. Tel: (079 83) 3305

🍺 🍺 🍺 🍺 🍺 🍺 🍺

NUTHURST

Situated in the thickly-wooded Weald, four miles south of Horsham, yet still remaining remote. A delightful terrace of cottages contains the village pub.
Population: 1,530.

PUBLIC HOUSE

The Black Horse

Nuthurst Street. Tel: (040 376) 272

🍺 🍺 🍺 🍺 🍺 🍺 🍺

NYETIMBER

A tiny hamlet on the flat coastal plain, west of Bognor, gradually becoming engulfed by creeping urbanization. One or two old cottages remain.

RESTAURANT

The Inglenook Hotel & Restaurant
255 Pagham Road. Tel: (0243) 262495

🍺 🍺 🍺 🍺 🍺 🍺 🍺

NYEWOOD

A hamlet consisting of one street in the wooded countryside north of the Hartings.

OTHER AMENITY

TAXI
Safe Travel
Prestwood. Tel: (073 080) 712

🍺 🍺 🍺 🍺 🍺 🍺 🍺

OVING

For many years this rural village west of Chichester was without a pub, now it has not only one of the most popular and pleasant pubs in the whole area, but also boasts its own brewery.
Population: 904.

PUBLIC HOUSE

The Gribble Inn
Tel: (0243) 786893

🍺 🍺 🍺 🍺 🍺 🍺 🍺

PAGHAM

Pagham Harbour is a large natural harbour, largely silted up and inaccessible to ships. But man's loss is nature's gain, and the harbour is now a bird sanctuary, and one of the wildest and remotest places in this heavily built-up region. The road that leads to the harbour is alongside the Norman church, dedicated to St Thomas à Becket, and built a few years after his death. Pagham itself spawns estates of bungalows with alarming rapidity.
Population: 5,028.

HOTELS

The Kings Beach Hotel
Sea Lane. Tel: (0243) 262006/262337

The Lion Hotel & Country Club
Nyetimber Lane. Tel: (0243) 262149
The Millstone Cottage Hotel
Church Lane. Tel: (0243) 263433

RESTAURANTS
Cardinals Restaurant
170 Pagham Road. Tel: (0243) 264911
China Garden
20 Rose Green Road. Tel: (0243) 267133
Knife & Fork
Nyetimber Lane. Tel: (0243) 264253
Pagham Fish Bar
164 Pagham Road. Tel: (0243) 264024

PUBLIC HOUSES
The Bear Inn
237 Pagham Road. Tel: (0243) 262157
The Lamb Inn
Pagham Road. Tel: (0243) 262168
The Lion Hotel
Nyetimber Lane. Tel: (0243) 262149

CAFES & TEA ROOMS
Church Farm Cafeteria
Church Farm Caravan Site, Pagham Road.
Tel: (0243) 265819
Pagham Beach Cafe
1 Beach Road. Tel: (0243) 267433

OTHER AMENITIES
CARAVAN PARKS
Church Farm Holiday Village
Tel: (0243) 262635
Copthorne Caravans
Rose Green Road. Tel: (0243) 262408
Mill Farm Caravan Park
259 Pagham Road. Tel: (0243) 262321

FLORISTS
Barbara's
9 The Parade. Tel: (0243) 263819

LIBRARY
Willowhale Library
84 Pryors Lane. Tel: (0243) 265712

🐾 🐾 🐾 🐾 🐾 🐾 🐾

PARTRIDGE GREEN
An agricultural 19th century settlement north of
Henfield.

HOTEL

The Partridge Hotel
Church Road. Tel: (0403) 710391

PUBLIC HOUSE
Green Man
Jolesfield. Tel: (0403) 710250

OTHER AMENITY
CARAVAN PARK
Wincaves Caravan Park
Honeybridge Lane. Tel: (0403) 710923

🐾 🐾 🐾 🐾 🐾 🐾 🐾

PATCHING
A small downland village just north of the main
A27 coastal road north-west of Worthing, grouped
with Clapham. There are a few old flint and
thatched cottages, and an Early English church.
Population: 208.

PUBLIC HOUSES
The Fox Inn
Arundel Road. Tel: (090 674) 337
The Fox is on the A27 with a large garden for children.
*Brewery: Phoenix. Licensee: Mr Julian Barrett. Beer available:
Traditional beers and lager. Garden. Car Park.*
Horse & Groom Inn
Arundel Road. Tel: (090 674) 346

🐾 🐾 🐾 🐾 🐾 🐾 🐾

PEASE POTTAGE
Known to many Brighton-bound travellers on the
M23 by its signpost, this must be one of the strang-
est place names in Sussex.

RESTAURANT
Pilgrims Of Cottesmore
Cottesmore Golf Club, Buchan Hill. Tel: (0293) 23667

PUBLIC HOUSE
The Grapes Inn
Brighton Road. Tel: (0293) 26359

🐾 🐾 🐾 🐾 🐾 🐾 🐾

PETWORTH
For miles before one reaches Petworth from the
north, the road runs parallel to a stone wall, punc-
tuated periodically by Lodge Gates, that actually
marks the perimeter of the grounds of Petworth
House. Once in the town, the wall doubles in size,
and the road snakes its way around it. Petworth

65

CANADIAN GEESE AT THE BOATING LAKE AT PETWORTH HOUSE

House dominates this charming country town, unfortunately not designed for the traffic that clogs it up, especially in the summer. There are fine old buildings everywhere, and inviting pubs and restaurants. On the north wall of the Town Hall was a bust of William III, sadly now removed. Petworth is a town where the visitor can spend a long time exploring lanes and footpaths, finding something interesting round every corner.
Population: 2,947.

PLACES OF INTEREST
Petworth House
Tel: (0798) 42476
Late 17th century house. Important collection of pictures (many by Turner & Van Dyck) sculpture & furniture, carving by Grinling Gibbons. Set in beautiful deer park. *Months Open: April to end October. Days Open: Daily except Monday and Friday. Hours Open: House; 1-5pm. Gardens and car park 12.30-5pm. Bank Holidays: Open Good Friday & Bank Holiday Monday. Admission: £3. Children Half price. Extra rooms open Tues, Wed, Thurs. Shop 1-5pm.*

RESTAURANTS
The Cellar
Swan House , Market Square. Tel: (0798) 42423
Goodwill Restaurant and Takeaway

Tel: (0798) 42922
Paddingtons Table
Tel: (0798) 43149
Soanes
Tel: (0798) 43659
Tudor Cottage Restaurant
Saddlers Row. Tel: (0798) 42125

PUBLIC HOUSES
The Angel Hotel
Angel Street.
Badger & Honeyjar
Station Road. Tel: (0798) 43559
Masons Arms
North Street. Tel: (0798) 42510
Well Diggers Arms
Pulborough Road. Tel: (0798) 42287

CAFE/TEA ROOMS
The Lamp Coffee Shop
Lombard Street. Tel: (0798) 45538

OTHER AMENITIES
ART GALLERY
Howes Gallery
Market Square. Tel: (0798) 43523

CAR HIRE
Empire Garage
Station Road. Tel: (0798) 42288/42868

TAXI
Petworth Private Hire Taxis
4, Meadow Way. Tel: (0798) 42691
Private Hire (Taxi)
Months Open: All. Days Open: 7 days a week. Hours Open: 24
hours. Bank Holidays open: All. Airports, weddings, day trips,
any occasion, any distance. Monthly accounts arranged. Ad-
vance bookings welcomed. Seven- seaters available.   Proprie-
tor: Mr ER Ireland.

PLAISTOW
A village set in a clearing in the woods of the Weald, with some pretty brick and tile-hung cottages, and a Victorian church.
Population: 1,753.

HOTEL
The Bush Inn
Rickmans Lane. Tel: (040 388) 246

PUBLIC HOUSE
The Sun Inn
The Street. Tel: (040 388) 313

POUND HILL
One of the original villages that make up the present day New Town of Crawley.

HOTEL
Barnwood Hotel
Balcombe Road. Tel: (0293) 882709

PUBLIC HOUSES
Parson's Pig
Balcombe Road. Tel: (0293) 883104
Tavern On The Green
Grattons Drive. Tel: (0293) 882468
Free house. Licensee: Mr M F Monaghan. Beer available: Real
ales, assorted lagers, keg bitter, cider. Garden. Childrens room. Car
Park.
The White Knight
Worth Road. Tel: (0293) 513197

OTHER AMENITIES
CAR HIRE
Elite Chauffeur Service

PETWORTH

Worth Corner, Turners Hill Road. Tel: (0293) 885555
Gatwick Minidrive
55, Burns Road. Tel: (0293) 23745
Hire Drive Services
14 Grattons Drive. Tel: (0293) 516912

POYNINGS
A pretty little village tucked under the northern escarpment of the downs, below Devil's Dyke. One of the modern aerial sights is of hang-gliders floating above, launched from the downs.
Population: 267.

PUBLIC HOUSES
The Inn At Devils Dyke
Dyke Road. Tel: (079 156) 256
The Royal Oak
The Street. Tel: (079 156) 389

RESTAURANT
Yat Sum House
9, Parade East. Tel: (0903) 785339

PRINSTED
A tiny unspoilt village on Chichester Harbour, totally unaffected by the main coastal road that passes just to the north. Some of the prettiest cottages on the Sussex coast are to be found on the Y-shaped layout of lanes that lead down to the harbour.

PUBLIC HOUSE
The Harvest Home
Main Road. Tel: (0243) 379138

OTHER AMENITY
MARINA

67

Thornham Marina
Thornham Lane. Tel: (0243) 375335

🐏 🐏 🐏 🐏 🐏 🐏 🐏

PULBOROUGH

Standing at the conference of the Rivers Arun and Rother, and also on the crossroads of the London-Chichester, and Winchester-Brighton road, Pulborough itself is a cross between a town and village. The modern town runs parallel with the Arun, crossed now by a bridge by-passing the old, narrower bridge. A pleasant place.

Population: 4,050.

HOTELS
The Arun Hotel
Lower Street. Tel: (079 82) 2162
Chequers Hotel
Church Place. Tel: (079 82) 2486

RESTAURANTS
Bonnies Restaurant and Tea Rooms
72, Lower Street. Tel: (079 82) 3244
Pulborough Tandoori Restaurant
2, Ferrymead Station Road. Tel: (079 82) 3570
Stane Street Hollow Restaurant
Tel: (079 82) 2819
The Waters Edge
Tel: (079 82) 2451

PUBLIC HOUSES
The Five Bells
6 / 7, London Road.Tel: (079 82) 2288
The Oddfellows Arms Hotel
Lower Street. Tel: (079 82) 3766
The Red Lion
145, Lower Street.Tel: (079 82) 2659
Rose & Crown
Stane Street, Codmore Hill.Tel: (079 82) 2663
The Swan
Station Road. Tel: (079 82) 3082
The White Horse Inn
Mare Hill. Tel: (079 82) 2189

OTHER AMENITIES
GARDEN CENTRE
Murrells Garden Centre
Broomers Hill Lane. RH20 2DU Tel: (079 82) 5508

TAXI
Star Cars
Station Road. Tel: (079 82) 2952
A-Z Taxis

Lizpah West, Chiltington Road. Tel: (079 82) 3230

GARDEN CENTRE
Nightingales Garden Centre
Codmore Hill. Tel: (079 82) 5122

🐏 🐏 🐏 🐏 🐏 🐏 🐏

PYECOMBE

A small downland village north of Brighton. Famous in the 19th century for its Pyecombe Hooks, or shepherd's crooks.

Population: 258.

PUBLIC HOUSE
Plough Inn
London Road. Tel: (079 18) 2796

🐏 🐏 🐏 🐏 🐏 🐏 🐏

ROFFEY

A suburb north-west of Horsham, on the edge of St Leonard's Forest, consisting mostly of Victorian terraces.

PUBLIC HOUSE
The Star Inn
Crawley Road. Tel: (0403) 59890

OTHER AMENITY
TAXI
Horsham Taxis
10, Moorhead Road. Tel: (0403) 54448

🐏 🐏 🐏 🐏 🐏 🐏 🐏

ROGATE

A charming village close to the Hampshire border, on the River Rother. The name is said to be derived from the gate where roe deer passed into the forest. A pretty group of sandstone cottages and the 13th century church of St Bartholomew are located at the main crossroads.

Population: 1,459.

PLACES OF INTEREST
Durford Heath
A 62 acre expanse of heathland, owned by the National Trust.

PUBLIC HOUSES
The White Horse
East Street. Tel: (073 080) 333
The Wyndham Arms

North Street. Tel: (073 080) 315

🐦 🐦 🐦 🐦 🐦 🐦 🐦

ROSE GREEN

A village situated between Bognor Regis and Pagham, largely consisting of estates of bungalows.

🐦 🐦 🐦 🐦 🐦 🐦 🐦

ROWHOOK

A hamlet close to the Surrey border, located at an old road junction of Stane Street and the Roman road to Guildford.

PUBLIC HOUSE

Chequers Inn
Tel: (0403) 790480

🐦 🐦 🐦 🐦 🐦 🐦 🐦

RUDGWICK

In the Weald north-west of Horsham; the church, Holy Trinity, is only yards from the Surrey border. Attractive tile-hung cottages screen the church from the road.
Population: 2,236.

RESTAURANT

L'Antico Restaurant
Tel: (040 372) 2446

PUBLIC HOUSES

The Blue Ship
The Haven. Tel: (040 372) 2706
Fox Inn
Bucks Green. Tel: (040 372) 2386
The Kings Head
Church Hill. Tel: (040 372) 2200
The Mucky Duck
Tismans Common. Tel: (040 372) 2300
Queens Head
Bucks Green. Tel: (040 372) 2202
Wheatsheaf Inn
Ellens Green. Tel: (040 372) 2155

OTHER AMENITY

TAXI
Rudgwick Car Hire
8, Kilnfield Road. Tel: (040 372) 2545

🐦 🐦 🐦 🐦 🐦 🐦 🐦

RUNCTON

A village on the flat coastal plain south of Chichester, with corn fields, nurseries and the downs to the north in the background.

OTHER AMENITIES

GARDEN CENTRES
Freshacres Nurseries
Manor Nursery, Lagness Road. Tel: (0243) 788222
Hill Brothers
Lagness Road. Tel: (0243) 787152
Manor Nurseries
Plant Centre/Garden Shop, Lagness Road. Tel: (0243) 781734

🐦 🐦 🐦 🐦 🐦 🐦 🐦

RUSPER

A tiny unspoilt village (except for the roar of the jets from Gatwick Airport) in beautiful countryside north of Horsham, so close to the Surrey border that it seems more like a Surrey village. The bellows attached to the Star Inn are all that remain of the old forge. *Population: 2,657.*

HOTELS

Ghyll Manor Hotel
High Street. Tel: (029 384) 571
The Lamb Inn
Lambs Green. Tel: (029 384) 336

PUBLIC HOUSES

Plough Inn
High Street. Tel: (029 384) 312
Royal Oak
Friday Street. Tel: (029 384) 393
The Star Inn
Horsham Road. Tel: (029 384) 264

🐦 🐦 🐦 🐦 🐦 🐦 🐦

RUSTINGTON

A residential suburb east of Littlehampton, right on the sea. Although there are few old houses, there are many pleasant housing estates and Rustington is an attractive and sought-after place to live.
Population: 9,568.

HOTEL

Mayday Hotel
12, Broadhurst Lane. Tel: (0903) 771198

GUEST HOUSES

Cranleigh Guest house
67, Broadmark lane. Tel: (0903) 785449

Kenmore Guest House
Claigmar Road. Tel: (0903) 784634
Luxury guest house in quiet garden setting near beach and shops. B&B self catering facilities.
Months Open: All year. Number of Bedrooms: 7. (4 with bathroom). B&B per person: £19.25. TV in rooms. Pets. 7 space car park. Garden. Proprietor: Mr R.L. Shaw

RESTAURANTS

The Copper Pot
1, Broadmark Parade. Tel: (0903) 786244

Simon's Restaurant
5, Sterling Parade. Tel: (0903) 770925

Wedgies
35, Sea Lane. Tel: (0903) 786235

PUBLIC HOUSES

Lamb Inn
Tel: (0903) 783227

The Smugglers Roost
125, Sea Lane.Tel: (0903) 785714

CAFE/TEA ROOMS

Chris's Coffee
Windmill Parade, Worthing Road. Tel: (0903) 782868

OTHER AMENITIES

CAR HIRE
A. C. Car Hire
Sea Lane. Tel: (0903) 772047

Blue Car Hire
Broadmark Lane. Tel: (0903) 782087

GARDEN CENTRES
D. Combes
Tel: (0903) 776274

Lowertrees Plant centre
Roundstone By Pass. Tel: (0903) 770457

STORE
Woolworths
15 Churchill Parade, The Street. Tel: (0903) 786320

TAXI
Black Knight Taxis
Station Aproach, Angmering Station. Tel: (0903) 786536

ð¬ ð¬ ð¬ ð¬ ð¬ ð¬ ð¬

SCAYNES HILL

South-east of Haywards Heath, Scaynes Hill con-

sists of a few houses and a 19th century church close to the border with East Sussex.

PUBLIC HOUSES

Farmers Inn
Lewes Road. Tel: (044 486) 419

The Sloop Inn
Sloop Lane. Tel: (044 486) 219

OTHER AMENITIES

GARDEN CENTRE
Scaynes Hill Nursery
Anchor Hill. Tel: (044 486) 673

HEALTH CLUB
Brighton Sun Club
Sloop Lane. RH17 7NP Tel: (044 486) 675

ð¬ ð¬ ð¬ ð¬ ð¬ ð¬ ð¬

SELHAM

Set in glorious countryside east of Midhurst on the River Rother; scattered tile-hung, stone and brick houses. St James' is a Saxon church.

HOTEL

The Three Moles Inn
Tel: (079 85) 303

ð¬ ð¬ ð¬ ð¬ ð¬ ð¬ ð¬

SELSEY

Selsey Bill, the most southern peninsular west of the Isle of Wight used to jut even further out into the English Channel before coastal erosion took place. Vast sea walls have now been built to stop this erosion. An important Saxon town, and once the diocese of a Saxon bishop, there has long been a legend that there is a cathedral under the sea, which is probably true. The main road goes straight down to the coast, to abruptly stop with no promenade or pier. Selsey is a popular seaside resort, and home to one of the busiest lifeboats on the South Coast.
Population: 7,540.

HOTELS

The Cottage Guest House
113 High Street. Tel: (0243) 605413

Rushmere House Hotel
Hillfield Road. Tel: (0243) 602612

Seal Hotel
6 Hillfield Road. Tel: (0243) 602461

SELSEY'S LIFEBOAT, ONE OF THE BUSIEST ON THE SOUTH COAST

GUEST HOUSES

Four Seasons Guest House
63 Hillfield Road. Tel: (0243) 604697

Norton Lea Guest House
Chichester Road. Tel: (0243) 605454

RESTAURANTS

Den's Fish Shop
163 High Street. Tel: (0243) 605467

Greg's Licensed Restaurant
92 High Street. Tel: (0243) 602682

Riviera Restaurant
3 New Shopping Parade, High Street. Tel: (0243) 603427

Selsey Indian Tandoori Restaurant
3/3a Hillfield Road. Tel: (0243) 602243/605799

The Stargazer
Manor Road. Tel: (0243) 602317

The Village
144 High Street. Tel: (0243) 605215

PUBLIC HOUSES

The Crown Inn
High Street. Tel: (0243) 602123

The Fisherman's Joy
71 East Street. Tel: (0243) 602121

The Lifeboat
Albion Road. Tel: (0243) 603501

The Selsey Bill
83 Hillfield Road. Tel: (0243) 602641

The Stargazer
Manor Road. Tel: (0243) 602317

CAFES & TEA ROOMS

The Gannet
High Street. Tel: (0243) 605121

Jeannie's Cafe
141 High Street. Tel: (0243) 602867

Munchies
High Street. Tel: (0243) 602780

OTHER AMENITIES

CAR HIRE/CHAUFFEUR DRIVE

Selsey Taxis
34 Park Lane. Tel: (0243) 604467

Weltax
111 High Street. Tel: (0243) 602761

CARAVAN PARKS

Bisquit Club
Montalon Crescent, Mill Lane. Tel: (0243) 602315

E.F. Hobbs
2 Manor Lane. Tel: (0243) 602601

The Nook Caravan Park
Site Office, Warners Lane. Tel: (0243) 602683

West Sands Caravan Park
Mill Lane. Tel: (0243) 602996/602654

White Horse Caravans
Paddock Lane. Tel: (0243) 604121/604915

71

FLORISTS
Village Flowers
129 High Street. Tel: (0243) 602863

HOLIDAY CAMP
Little Spain Holiday Homes
Golf Links Lane. Tel: (0243) 602165/602159/602958

LIBRARY
Selsey Library
School Lane. Tel: (0243) 602096

ᔆᔆ ᔆᔆ ᔆᔆ ᔆᔆ ᔆᔆ ᔆᔆ ᔆᔆ

SHERMANBURY

Just north of Henfield, an urban settlement with a medieval church, St Giles.
Population: 425.

OTHER AMENITY
TAXI
PVT. Car Hire
Woodside, Brighton Road. GU2 0LF Tel: (0403) 710975

ᔆᔆ ᔆᔆ ᔆᔆ ᔆᔆ ᔆᔆ ᔆᔆ ᔆᔆ

SHIPLEY

Shipley is in the Weald, south of Horsham, yet in sight of the downs, on the River Adur. The home of

the poet and lover of windmills Hilaire Belloc (see Halnaker), Shipley has a fine early 19th century windmill, and an interesting church, St Mary, founded by the Knights Templar in 1125.
Population: 1,219.

PUBLIC HOUSE
The Countryman
Whitehall. Tel: (040 387) 383
Traditional country pub/restaurant with fine wines, traditional ales, home made food, fresh fish and local game.
Free house. Opening Hours: 11.00-3.00, 5.30-11.00. Beer available: traditional ales, Stella Artois, Heineken, Guinness. Food available: 12.00-2.00, 7.00-9.30. Specialities: fresh fish, local game. Garden. Car Park.

GUEST HOUSE
G.A. Williams
Park House Green Lane . Tel: (0293) 786806

OTHER AMENITY
CAR HIRE
A & P Car Hire
Shipley Bridge. Tel: (0293) 786168

ᔆᔆ ᔆᔆ ᔆᔆ ᔆᔆ ᔆᔆ ᔆᔆ ᔆᔆ

SHOREHAM-BY-SEA

Shoreham has been a port for centuries, and became much busier after the River Adur silted up in the Middle Ages, and ships couldn't get upstream to Bramber. It is still the biggest commercial harbour between Southampton and Dover, an inland lagoon dominated by the huge power station that is built on a strip of land parallel to the harbour's mouth. Shoreham has a pretty High Street, with some interesting buildings and old inns, including one with a ship's figurehead outside, and has two magnificent Norman churches, St Nicholas and St Mary de Haura (de Havre). Inigo Jones was Member of Parliament here in 1620. A new bridge to the north has taken much of the traffic out of the town, allowing locals to go about their business in peace. Shoreham Airport serves both Brighton and Worthing.

PLACES OF INTEREST
Marlipins Museum
Tel: (0273) 462994

RESTAURANTS
The Dolphin Restaurant
13, Buckingham Road. Tel: (0273) 453559
The Gallery Restaurant

SHOREHAM HARBOUR

22b, East Street. Tel: (0273) 763389
The Indian Cottage Restaurant
76, High Street. Tel: (0273) 453379
La Gondola
90, High Street. Tel: (0273) 463231
Marinas Restaurant
21, Ferry Road. Tel: (0273) 463476
The New Amsterdam
467/471, Upper Shoreham Road. Tel: (0273) 455055
The New Taj Tandoori
276a, Upper Shoreham Road . Tel: (0273) 455069
<R Title>Palm Court Coffee Co
29/31, Ferry Road. Tel: (0273) 464768
The Royal Coach
Tel: (0273) 454077
Welcome House
32, Kingston Broadway. Tel: (0273) 591701

PUBLIC HOUSES
The Bridge Hotel
87, High Street.Tel: (0273) 452477
The Buckingham Arms
Brunswick Road. Tel: (0273) 453660
Burrel Arms Hotel
Brunswick Road. Tel: (0273) 452023
Crabtree Inn
6, Buckingham Road.Tel: (0273) 463508
The Duke of Wellington
368, Brighton Road.Tel: (0273) 465275
Ferry Inn
1, East Street.Tel: (0273) 454125
The Green Jacket
Upper Shoreham Road. Tel: (0273) 452556
The Lady Jane
Lower Beach Road. Tel: (0273) 452902

Marlipins
High Street. Tel: (0273) 453369
Morning Star
Ham Road. Tel: (0273) 453407
Red Lion Inn
Old Shoreham Road. Tel: (0273) 453171
The Royal Sovereign
Middle Street. Tel: (0273) 452527
Rumours
49a, Grove Road.Tel: (0273) 453518
Schooner Inn
64, High Street.Tel: (0273) 452527
The Surrey Arms
388, Brighton Road.Tel: (0273) 452220
Swiss Cottage
Old Shoreham Road. Tel: (0273) 453301

CAFE/TEA ROOMS
The Cuckoo Clock
74, High Street. Tel: (0273) 453853

OTHER AMENITIES
BUS & COACH SERVICES
Brighton & Hove Bus & Coach Company
86, High Street. Tel: (0273) 452086

CAR HIRE
Arun Radio Cabs
Little High Street. Tel: (0273) 461359/461395
Intacar
Unit 5 , Ham Business Centre. Tel: (0273) 454023
Keen & Betts
Brighton Road. Tel: (0273) 461333
Prestige Car Hire
202, Brighton Road. Tel: (0273) 453382

GARDEN CENTRES

B. T. Edmonds
Eastern Avenue. Tel: (0273) 461999
Sandel Perkins
Malthouse Trading Estate, Brighton Road. Tel: (0273) 596546
Shoreham Garden Shop
417, Upper Shoreham Road . Tel: (0273) 453218

STORE

Woolworths
56, High Street. Tel: (0273) 452858

TAXIS

ABCA Taxis
Stills Yard, 17 Riverside Road. Tel: (0273) 452828/453003
Access Cars
82a, High Street. Tel: (0273) 452424
Bel-Cabs
Station Aproach. Tel: (0273) 454455
Ranks
Shoreham Station. Tel: (0273) 453003
Richard's Taxis Service
7, Cissbury Way. Tel: (0273) 464547
Southern Taxis
Shoreham Airport. Tel: (0273) 461655

WATER SPORTS

The Adur Water Activities Centre
Brighton Road. Tel: (0273) 462928

ﻌﺎ ﻌﺎ ﻌﺎ ﻌﺎ ﻌﺎ ﻌﺎ ﻌﺎ

SHRIPNEY

A village known locally for its by-pass leading motorists into Bognor Regis. There are several large caravan estates in the area, so naturally enough the population is much larger in the summer than at other times.

PUBLIC HOUSE

Robin Hood Inn
Shripney Road. Tel: (0243) 822323

OTHER AMENITIES

CAR HIRE/CHAUFFEUR DRIVE
A.L.P. Smith
Royce Cottage, Shripney Road. Tel: (0243) 865788

CARAVAN PARK

Marigolds Caravan Park
Shripney Road. Tel: (0243) 865876

ﻌﺎ ﻌﺎ ﻌﺎ ﻌﺎ ﻌﺎ ﻌﺎ ﻌﺎ

SIDLESHAM

A delightful little village between Chichester and Selsey, that is located on a creek of Pagham Harbour. The main street has some pretty thatched cottages, and a welcoming village pub.
Population: 1,185.

RESTAURANT

Blackfords Restaurant
Mill Lane. Tel: (024 356) 531

PUBLIC HOUSES

Anchor Inn
Selsey Road. Tel: (024 356) 373
Crab & Lobster
Mill Lane. Tel: (024 356) 233
Pagham Harbour Local Nature Reserve
The Ferry, Selsey Road. Tel: (024 356) 508

CAR HIRE/SELF DRIVE

Jury Car Hire
Jury Lane. Tel: (024 356) 230

ﻌﺎ ﻌﺎ ﻌﺎ ﻌﺎ ﻌﺎ ﻌﺎ ﻌﺎ

SINGLETON

Singleton is set in a beautiful location at the foot of the downs near Goodwood. Flint houses line the village lanes, and in the Saxon church, that has views up to the Trundle, there is a lepers' window (where lepers could receive communion without infecting anybody else). At the Lavant end of the village there is a delightfully situated cricket field alongside the local post-office.
Population: 490.

PLACES OF INTEREST

Weald & Downland Open Air Museum
Tel: (024 363) 348
The first museum in the country to re-erect and preserve old rural buildings. Exhibits include a forge, a blacksmiths and a pottery.
Months Open: All year. Days Open: Monday to Sunday. Hours Open: 11am-6pm (summer); 11am-4pm (winter). Bank Holidays: open. Admission: £2.80 OAPs £2.20. Children £1.25. Family ticket for two adults and two children £7.50.

PUBLIC HOUSES

Fox & Hounds
Tel: (024 363) 251
The Horse & Groom
Tel: (024 363) 282

ﻌﺎ ﻌﺎ ﻌﺎ ﻌﺎ ﻌﺎ ﻌﺎ ﻌﺎ

THE FOLLY NEAR SLINDON

SLAUGHAM

A pretty Wealden village to the south of Horsham, with the houses and restored Norman church grouped around a triangular green. The village has the interesting distinction of having no telephone wires, because in 1937 the then Lord of the Manor paid to have them laid underground. *Population: 3,893.*

HOTEL

The Chequers Inn

Tel: (0444) 400239

Set in the prettiest village in Sussex the Chequers offers luxury rooms and a fine restaurant and bar menu, specialising in seafood.

BEDROOMS: 6 Double, (6 en suite, 6 TV, 6 phone, 6 tea/coffee) B&B £47.00 - £55.00. RESTAURANT: Fish & English Fayre. Lunch: £15.00. À La Carte: £16.00. Specialities: Seafood. Credit Cards: Ac. Am. D. V.

RIGHT. THE CHEQUERS INN, SLAUGHAM

SLINDON

A brick and flint village now preserved by the National Trust. Built on the slopes of the downs in a quiet position just off the A29, there is a quadrant of lanes, a restored 11th century church, and Slindon House, once the palace of the Archbishops of Canterbury. Slindon woods are a delightful place to see bluebells in Spring. *Population: 503.*

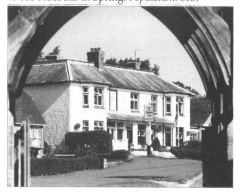

ST MARY'S CHURCH AT SOMPTING IS ONE OF THE MOST IMPORTANT SAXON CHURCHES IN THE COUNTRY

PUBLIC HOUSES

Newburgh Arms
School Hill. Tel: (024 365) 229

The Spur
London Road. Tel: (024 365) 216

🦆 🦆 🦆 🦆 🦆 🦆 🦆

SLINDON COMMON

CAFE/TEA ROOMS

The Fair Mile Cafe
Fair Mile Bottom, Madehurst. Tel: (024 365) 505

🦆 🦆 🦆 🦆 🦆 🦆 🦆

SLINFOLD

Slinfold is just off the main A29 Stane Street, due
west of Horsham. A carefully preserved Wealden
village, with a good mixture of old and new dwell-
ings.

Population: 1,650.

HOTEL

Random Hall Hotel
Stane Street. RH13 7QX. Tel: (024 365) 790558

OTHER AMENITY

CARAVAN PARK

Caravan Club
The Old Station. Tel: (024 365) 790269

🦆 🦆 🦆 🦆 🦆 🦆 🦆

SMALL DOLE

A tiny village north of the Adur Gap through the
downs, just south of Henfield.

PLACES OF INTEREST

New Hall
Tel: (0273) 492546

RESTAURANT

Golding Barn Restaurant
Tel: (0903) 813344

PUBLIC HOUSE

Fox & Hounds
Henfield Road. Tel: (0273) 492850

OTHER AMENITIES

CAR HIRE

Kestrel Private Car Hire Service
Chanctonbury, Wood Lane. Tel: (0273) 492940

CARAVAN PARK

Southdown Caravan Park
Henfield Road. Tel: (0903) 814323

🦆 🦆 🦆 🦆 🦆 🦆 🦆

SOMPTING

St Mary's church at Sompting is one of the most
important Saxon churches in the country, one of
only a handful of buildings that survive from the
10th century. The Knights Templar rebuilt the
church in 1184, leaving the tower. The Templars
fell from grace amidst rumours of black magic, to
be replaced by the Knights Hospitallers, who ex-
tended the church. The village of Sompting, separated from the church by the busy A27, has become
a suburb of Worthing. The lane past the church
goes up over the downs to Steyning, a five-mile
walk for the energetic.
Population: 8,512.

RESTAURANT

Smugglers Restaurant
West Street. Tel: (0903) 36072

PUBLIC HOUSES

Ball Tree Inn
Tel: (0903) 753090

The Joyful Whippet
Halewick Lane. Tel: (0903) 753900

Marquis Of Branby
West Street. Tel: (0903) 31102

OTHER AMENITY

CAR HIRE

William Weller & Son
West Street. Tel: (0903) 762371

🦆 🦆 🦆 🦆 🦆 🦆 🦆

SOUTH HARTING

Approached from Petersfield to the north-west,
South Harting is seen picturesquely huddled up
beneath a wooded part of the South Downs. It was
the prospect of climbing the steep Harting Hill to
reach Uppark that dissuaded the Duke of Wellington from buying the great house, when he said
"I've crossed the Alps once". The church and houses
of the town grouped around are as charming close
up as they are from afar, and there are some good
inns and red brick Georgian houses on its wide
High Street. The author Anthony Trollope lived
and died here, and his writing implements are
preserved in a case in the church, unusually dedi-

A WOODED PART OF THE SOUTH DOWNS AT SOUTH HARTING

cated to St Mary and St Gabriel, that dominates the southern part of the village.

PLACES OF INTEREST

Uppark
Tel: (0730) 825317
Now sadly damaged by fire, this magnificent 17th century house has associations with Lady Hamilton, Nelson's lover, and with H.G. Wells, whose mother was housekeeper here. *(See feature opposite.)*

PUBLIC HOUSES

Coach & Horses
Tel: (0730) 825229
The Ship Inn
Tel: (0730) 825302
The White Hart
Tel: (0730) 825355

OTHER AMENITY

ART GALLERY
For Arts Sake
The Square. Tel: (0730) 825726

SOUTHBOURNE

The coastal road between Chichester and the Hampshire border at Emsworth is mostly built-up all the way, and one village tends to merge into the next, but Southbourne has St John's church right on the road to distinguish it. To the south there are several lanes that run down to Chichester Harbour.
Population: 5,789.

SOUTHGATE

One of the original parishes that has been swallowed up by the New Town of Crawley.

HOTEL

Barrington Hotel
Hunter Road. Tel: (0293) 26038

GUEST HOUSE

Westoe
128, Malthouse Road. Tel: (0293) 24189

PUBLIC HOUSE

The Downsman
Wakehurst Drive. Tel: (0293) 26173

OTHER AMENITY

TAXI
Express Cars
14a, Springfield Road. Tel: (0293) 514483

UPPARK - A PHOENIX FROM THE ASHES
by Lawrence Rich

HIGH ON THE SUSSEX DOWNS stands the most romantic of country houses. Yet despite a terrible fire in 1989, Uppark is talked of in the present tense while it rises like a phoenix from the ashes.

It was built in 1690 for a very dubious character, Lord Grey of Werke. Eight years earlier he had run off with Lady Henrietta Berkeley, his own wife's sister, and received a severe drubbing in court when Lord Berkeley sued for her return. While still under thirty he was next indicted for high treason, over the Rye House Plot involving his close friend the Duke of Monmouth. Committed to the Tower, Grey arrived 'after the gates were shut', so got his guards drunk and slipping across the Thames rode fast for Uppark. There he and Henrietta had supper in the woods before taking ship to the Low Countries. Lord Grey took part in Monmouth's Rebellion, commanding the cavalry - disastrously - at Sedgemoor, was taken prisoner by James II and

stripped of his assets. But when James fled the country and William III was crowned, Grey's estates were returned, he built the present house and was created Earl of Tankerville.

In 1747 his family sold it. The buyer was Matthew Fetherstonhaugh, a young man who had inherited an immense fortune on the conditions that he acquired a baronetcy and an estate in southern England. Happily fulfilling these enticing terms, Sir Matthew married Sarah, daughter of a rich Middlesex merchant, and in their first year together they improved house and grounds to the tune of £100,000 - a very large sum at the time.

Most of the interior they transformed in the mid-18th-century taste. Creating the white and gold saloon, they introduced elaborate plasterwork, handpainted and flock wallpapers and their collections of furniture, books and objects d'art, with curtains and upholstery of the period and family

AFTER THE FIRE OF 31 AUGUST 1989

and Grand Tour paintings. Their Uppark exuded the spirit of the age.

In 1774 their son Harry, at twenty, succeeded to the title and estate. The lad's guardians included the Archbishop of Canterbury, but Sir Harry's disposition was more for extravagance than piety. He entertained lavishly, was a devotee of the turf and frequented the tables at Carlton House. Until 1810 he was an intimate of the Prince Regent until - like all close to the future king - they fell out. But Harry had inherited his parents' excellent taste, and he added china, French furniture from Paris and sporting pictures to Uppark.

At 26 he discovered a stunning young creature called Emma Hart, a country girl who was then a sort of showgirl in a London night club. Willingly exchanging this for the high life at Uppark, Emma is said to have danced for Harry's guests on the dining table, and she lived there over a year until being summarily packed off, six months pregnant. Befriended by Charles Greville, who had met her at an Uppark shooting party, Emma went on to her place among our national heroines. Sir William Hamilton married her, Nelson loved her, Romney painted her for her beauty; and thirty years on, when so much had changed, Sir Harry wrote compassionately to Lady Hamilton and more than

once settled her debts.

After Emma's departure Harry often entertained the Prince Regent at Uppark, laying on races, gastronomy and the cream of society. Then came the break with Prinny and Harry's retirement from society. But he never resigned his zest for life. In 1825, when over seventy, he married Mary Ann Bullock, his 20-year-old dairy maid and daughter of the Uppark park keeper. He had her educated in Paris, and they were happy for over twenty years until he died aged ninety-two in 1846. It is said that, when driving nearby one day a nosegay was tossed into Mary Ann's lap by a little girl at the roadside. "Who is that child?" asked Sir Harry, to be told "My little sister, Frances Bullock." "Then we'll have her up at the house and educate her." And so Uppark was to remain unchanged until the younger sister died a century and a half after its transformation by Harry's parents.

Yet two more characters are woven into the story - the Duke of Wellington and H.G.Wells. The former's defeat of Napoleon had him the darling of England, and Harry offered him the property when the Duke was house hunting in 1816. Uppark crowns a spur of downland so lofty that the distant Solent and Channel appear half-way up the sky when glimpsed to the south. One look at Uppark's steep approach warned the great soldier that his horses would need frequent changing. He turned the idea down saying, "I've crossed the Alps once."

On Mary Ann's death Frances Bullock took over and kept all "as Sir 'Arry 'ad it". She was helped by Miss Sutherland, her former governess who was whispered to be a natural daughter of Harry's. At this time H.G.Wells' mother was housekeeper, and here Wells stole his first 'downstairs' kiss. Its succession of long-lived custodians kept Uppark unchanged from the 1750s; and in 1895, when Frances died, the National Trust was born. Fifty years later the Fetherstonhaughs of the time presented the Trust with their wonderful home.

Fire always shocks for its remorseless indifference, and the loss of the roof was tragic. But nearly all the original contents were saved - all but one of the paintings, all moveable furniture, all the china, even textiles and curtains - and the ashes were minutely sifted in readiness for restoration. Moreover, the walls and chimneys all stand, and the showrooms, though damaged by debris, were not burned. Even plasterwork and chandeliers are capable of reassembly. Uppark's restoration repays a debt to all those whose passions had created and maintained it, and whose happiness charges the atmosphere.

SOUTHWATER

A hamlet that has been by-passed by a new stretch of the A24 Horsham-Worthing road, Southwater is an example of how old and new houses can co-exist harmoniously with one another.

PUBLIC HOUSES

Bax Castle
Two Mile Ash. Tel: (0403) 53128
Bridge House Inn
Copsdale . Tel: (0403) 730383
Cock Inn
Worthing Road. Tel: (0403) 730205
Hen & Chicken
Worthing Road. Tel: (0403) 730349

OTHER AMENITY

CAR HIRE
Cosmos Car Hire
12a The Gables , Shipley Corner. Tel: (0403) 731573

STAPLEFIELD

A large village green, with houses and the church of St Mark grouped around it, is the focal point of this village situated between Horsham and Haywards Heath.

HOTEL

The Jolly Tanners
Handcross Road. Tel: (0444) 400335

PUBLIC HOUSE

The Victory Inn
Warninglid Road. Tel: (0444) 400463

STEDHAM

A large village in the Rother valley west of Midhurst, with a street of brick and sandstone houses running down to the river, spanned by a six-arched 17th century bridge. St James' is built on the site of a Saxon church.
Population: 841.

PUBLIC HOUSE

The Hamilton
School Lane. Tel: (073 081) 2555

OTHER AMENITY

GARDEN CENTRE
Rotherhill Nurseries & Garden Centre
School Lane. Tel: (073 081) 3687

STEYNING

Steyning was once a royal manor owned by Alfred the Great, with its own mint. Located in a magnificent position at the foot of the downs, at the northern end of the Adur Gap, it was an important port in the days when the river was much wider and navigable (see Bramber). St. Andrew is one of the best examples of a Norman church in the county, if not the country. There are many fine buildings, from the 15th,16th and 17th centuries, like the famous Grammar School founded in 1614, and fine Georgian buildings too. Overall, Steyning is a very pleasant village, pleasant enough to entice Sir Lawrence Olivier to make his home here, until his death in 1989.
Population: 3,989.

PLACES OF INTEREST

Steyning Museum

HOTELS

Nash Hotel
Horsham Road. Tel: (0903) 814988
*BEDROOMS: 1 Single, (1 en suite, 1 TV, 1 tea/coffee) B&B £ 20.00 - £ 25.00. 1 Double, (1 TV, 1 tea/coffee) B&B £ 20.00 - £ 25.00. 3 Twin, (3 TV, 3 tea/coffee) B&B £ 20.00 - £ 25.00.
Recommendations: AA.*
Springwells Hotel
High Street. Tel: (0903) 812043

RESTAURANTS

Milestones
25, High St. Tel: (0903) 812338
Steyning House Restaurant
Tel: (0903) 812041

PUBLIC HOUSES

The Norfolk Arms
18, Church Street .Tel: (0903) 812215
The Star Inn
130, High Street.Tel: (0903) 813078
White Horse Inn
23, High Street.Tel: (0903) 812347

OTHER AMENITIES

ART GALLERY
The Gentle Gallery (See over)

STOPHAM BRIDGE, A MOST PHOTOGENIC SEVEN-ARCHED MEDIEVAL BRIDGE

The Gentle Gallery

94, High St. Tel: (0903) 812933

Art Gallery

Months Open: All. Days Open: Monday to Saturday. Hours Open: 9.00-1.00, 2.15-5.30. Picture framers, conservation framing and restoration. Anything framed. Fast efficient service. Large stocks of ready made frames. Gallery shows framed and unframed prints, limited editions, etching and originals. Many of local views. Fine selection of birthday and greetings cards. Proprietors: Messrs Basil & Nicholas Gentle.

STOPHAM

A most photogenic seven-arched medieval bridge, built in 1423, spans the River Arun, with a pub standing alongside it, making an ideal picture postcard. The village itself, between Pulborough and Petworth, has a Norman church and is built on a hilly cul-de-sac in some beautiful countryside. *Population: 86.*

PUBLIC HOUSE

The White Hart

Stopham Bridge. Tel: (079 82) 3321

🦋 🦋 🦋 🦋 🦋 🦋 🦋

STORRINGTON

A bustling main street forms the major part of Storrington. The church is part Norman, but no longer has the tall spire that was destroyed by lightning in 1731. The downs in the background have Celtic patterns preserved on their slopes. *Population: 3,775.*

CAR HIRE
Jubilee Cars Of Storrington
11, Hawthorn Way. Tel: (0903) 744717

🐚 🐚 🐚 🐚 🐚 🐚 🐚

PLACES OF INTEREST
Parham
Tel: (0903) 742021
A delightful Tudor House in a Tudor setting, including a characteristic 'chase' of trees and bracken. Fine collection of furniture, paintings and needlework including early Stewart stumpwork. 'Personal' tours via pre-recorded cassette hire.
Months Open: Easter Sunday - first Sunday in October. Days Open: Sunday, Wednesday, Thursday and Bank Holiday afternoons. Hours Open: Gardens & picnic area 1-6pm. House 2-6pm. Bank Holidays: All between Easter and October. Admission: £3. Children £1.50. OAPs £2.25.

HOTEL
The White Horse
2, The Square. Tel: (0903) 743451

RESTAURANTS
Cottage Tandoori
25, West Street. Tel: (0903) 743605
Manleys
Tel: (0903) 742331
Memories of Peking
25, Old Mill Square. Tel: (0903) 742919
The Old Forge Restaurant
6a, Church Street. Tel: (0903) 743402

PUBLIC HOUSES
The Anchor Inn & Restaurant
Tel: (0903) 742665
The Elephant & Castle
23, West Street.Tel: (0903) 745815
Half Moon
13, High Street.Tel: (0903) 744773

CAFE/TEA ROOMS
Willow Tea Room
5, Pulborough Road. Tel: (0903) 742600

OTHER AMENITIES
ART GALLERY
The Milligan Gallery
5 Eastbrook High St.. RH20 4BT Tel: (0903) 745031
Contemporary Art Gallery
Months Open: All year. Days Open: Tuesday to Saturday. Hours Open: 10.30-5.30. Proprietor: Fiona Milligan.

STOUGHTON
A village situated in a quiet valley in the downs north-west of Chichester, which consists of brick and flint barns and cottages. Bow Hill, at 677 feet, affords some wonderful views.
Population: 690.

PUBLIC HOUSE
Hare & Hounds
Tel: (0705) 631433

🐚 🐚 🐚 🐚 🐚 🐚 🐚

SUTTON
A quiet village just north of the downs, in delightful countryside. An interesting collection of buildings constructed from a variety of materials. The 14th century church has a Norman nave.
Population: 197.

PUBLIC HOUSE
The White Horse Inn
High Street . Tel: (079 87) 287

🐚 🐚 🐚 🐚 🐚 🐚 🐚

TANGMERE
East of Chichester on the coastal plain, the site of the famous Battle of Britain airfield, now disused. There is an interesting museum highlighting Tangmere's crucial role in the country's recent history. The village itself still suffers the ranks of RAF personnel houses, but there is a delightful 12th century church, St Andrew, and some fine old houses.
Population: 1,213.

PLACES OF INTEREST
Tangmere Military Aviation Museum
Tel: (0243) 775223

RESTAURANT
River Kwai Restaurant
Arundel Road (A27). Tel: (0243) 773294

PUBLIC HOUSE
Bader Arms
Malcolm Road. Tel: (0243) 779422

OTHER AMENITIES

CAR HIRE/CHAUFFEUR DRIVE
Peter Mellor Rolls Royces
30 Tangmere Road. Tel: (0243) 779002

TAXIS
Aaron Taxi Services
89 Cheshire Crescent. Tel: (0243) 774700
Taxi & Car & Bus Hire
Months Open: All. Days Open: Monday to Sunday. Hours Open: 24 hours. Bank Holidays: open. 5 cabs wheelchair accessible. Proprietor: Mr Ronald Hand.
Handicab Taxis & Car Hire
89 Cheshire Crescent. Tel: (0243) 779132
Taxi & Car & Bus Hire
Months Open: All. Days Open: Monday to Sunday. Hours Open: 24 hours. Bank Holidays: open. 5 wheelchair accessible cabs. Bus takes 11 passengers and 3 wheelchairs. Proprietor: Mr Ronald Hand.

❤ ❤ ❤ ❤ ❤ ❤

TARRING

A village that has been engulfed by Worthing, but by not being on a main road, has managed to retain some of its identity. Nearby is the remains of a palace belonging to the Archbishops of Canterbury during the 13th century, and the church too dates from that time.

RESTAURANTS
Ace Burgers
16, South Street. Tel: (0903) 38080
Akash Tandoori
62, South Street. Tel: (0903) 210597
The Parsonage
6/10, High Street. Tel: (0903) 820140

PUBLIC HOUSES
George & Dragon
High Street. Tel: (0903) 202497
The Vine Inn
High Street. Tel: (0903) 202891

CAFE/TEA ROOMS
Macari's Ice Cream Parlour
5, South Street. Tel: (0903) 34735

OTHER AMENITY
TAXI
A & B Taxis
26, South Street. Tel: (0903) 205557

❤ ❤ ❤ ❤ ❤ ❤ ❤

THAKEHAM

In the Weald, east of Pulborough, Thakeham is a quiet one-street village, surrounded by nurseries. Little Thakeham, just to the south, is one of the best houses designed by Lutyens in 1902. There are fine views from the churchyard of the downs to the south at Storrington.
Population: 1,565.

HOTEL
Little Thakeham
Merrywood Lane. Tel: (090 66) 4416

RESTAURANT
Abingworth Hall Hotel
Tel: (079 83) 3636

PUBLIC HOUSE
White Lion Inn
Street. Tel: (079 83) 3141

OTHER AMENITY
GARDEN CENTRE
June's Country Garden Shop
Storrrington Road . Tel: (090 66) 4504

❤ ❤ ❤ ❤ ❤ ❤ ❤

THREE BRIDGES

One of the parishes that make up the New Town of Crawley, and now absorbed by it.

RESTAURANT
Hillside Inn
Tel: (0293) 882146

CAFE/TEA ROOMS
Station Snack Bar
Railway Approach, Haslet Avenue. Tel: (0293) 519700

OTHER AMENITY
CAR HIRE
Crawley Car Repairs & Rentals
Stockwell Works , Stephenson Way. Tel: (0293) 542855

❤ ❤ ❤ ❤ ❤ ❤ ❤

TILGATE

Another of the parishes that was enveloped by Crawley.

RESTAURANT
Forest View Bar Restaurant
Tel: (0293) 545223

TILLINGTON

Just west of Petworth Park, and owned by the Estate, Tillington is built on a ridge above Petworth, with wonderful views to the south of the downs. A tidy, well-kept village full of character, and some fine buildings including the Manor House and some almshouses.

Population: 547.

PUBLIC HOUSE

Horseguards
Tel: (0798) 42332

🐾 🐾 🐾 🐾 🐾 🐾 🐾

TROTTON

Situated in the Rother valley on a bend in the river west of Midhurst, Trotton has a fine five-arched medieval bridge. In the 14th century St George's church there are two interesting brasses: one from 1310 depicts Lady Margaret Camoys, the oldest existing brass of a female , and the other is of Lord Thomas Camoys of 1419.

Population: 332.

HOTEL

Southdowns Hotel & Restaurant
Tel: (073 080) 521

PUBLIC HOUSE

The Keepers Arms
Tel: (073 081) 3724

OTHER AMENITY

GARDEN CENTRE
Aylings of Trotton
Tel: (073 081) 3621

🐾 🐾 🐾 🐾 🐾 🐾 🐾

TURNERS HILL

Turners Hill stands at 585 feet above sea level, in the countryside south east of Crawley, with a Victorian church at its peak.

HOTEL

Alexander House
Fen Place. Tel: (0342) 716333

PUBLIC HOUSE

The Red Lion
Lion Lane.

🐾 🐾 🐾 🐾 🐾 🐾 🐾

UPPER BEEDING

This village is located on the opposite side of the Adur Gap to Bramber, and consists mainly of one narrow main street lined with old cottages.

Population: 4,374.

PUBLIC HOUSE

Bridge Inn
High Street. Tel: (0903) 812773

OTHER AMENITY

CAR HIRE
Sovereign Private Hire
34, Manor Road. Tel: (0903) 814146

TAXI
Berwick & Dicher Taxi
The School House , Park Mead. Tel: (0323) 844302

🐾 🐾 🐾 🐾 🐾 🐾 🐾

WALBERTON

A pretty main street with a nice mixture of old and new buildings, predominantly flint, in the flat countryside north of Bognor Regis. Walberton House is an elegant early 19th century private house with an imposing drive. The church is on a Saxon site.

Population: 1,865.

HOTEL

Avisford Park Hotel
Yapton Lane. Tel: (0243) 551215

PUBLIC HOUSES

Holly Tree
The Street. Tel: (0243) 551497
The Royal Oak
Yapton Lane. Tel: (0243) 552865

OTHER AMENITIES

CAR HIRE/CHAUFFEUR DRIVE
Grainger of Walberton
8 Pound Road. Tel: (0243) 551572

GARDEN CENTRE
Jan de Vries
Strathmore Nursery, Eastergate Lane. Tel: (0243) 543022

🐾 🐾 🐾 🐾 🐾 🐾 🐾

WALDERTON

Situated in a peaceful unspoilt valley just below the downs north-west of Chichester, Walderton is a rural community. In the pub at the back is an old skittles alley.

PUBLIC HOUSE
The Barley Mow
Tel: (0705) 631321

🐦 🐦 🐦 🐦 🐦 🐦 🐦

WARNHAM

Close to the Surrey border, set in unspoilt countryside, Warnham is a village that has been preserved and cared for. St Margaret's is an essentially Victorian church with 16th century origins where the poet Shelley, native of Warnham, was baptised. *Population: 1,723.*

RESTAURANT
Tyldens Restaurant
Tel: (0403) 210424

PUBLIC HOUSES
Greets Inn
Friday Street. Tel: (0403) 65047
The Sussex Oak
2, Church Street.Tel: (0403) 65028

🐦 🐦 🐦 🐦 🐦 🐦 🐦

WARNINGCAMP

So called because it was the Romans' first line of defence in protecting Burpham, the old stronghold that lies at the end of this particular cul-de-sac. Warningcamp sits on a slight mound alongside the River Arun, across the flood plain from Arundel. The local flint is evident in the few houses and barns. *Population: 127.*

OTHER AMENITY
GARDEN CENTRE
Yeomans Nurseries
Tel: (0903) 883036

🐦 🐦 🐦 🐦 🐦 🐦 🐦

WARNINGLID

A Wealden hamlet south-west of Horsham, with a spear-carrying Saxon on the village sign.

RESTAURANT
Happy Eater Family Restaurant
Tel: (044 485) 239

PUBLIC HOUSE
Half Moon
The Street. Tel: (044 485) 227

OTHER AMENITY
TAXI
Andy's Taxis
Stanbridge View, London Road. Tel: (044 485) 266

🐦 🐦 🐦 🐦 🐦 🐦 🐦

WASHINGTON

Situated on a crossroads on the London-Worthing and Brighton-Petworth roads, at a precise spot where the Weald meets the downs. The houses are constructed of a variety of materials, sandstone, brick and flint. St Mary's, on top of the hill, has 12th century origins, and was rebuilt by the Victorians in 1867. *Population: 1,035.*

PLACES OF INTEREST
Chanctonbury Ring
An Iron Age hill fort with mystical connotations. The ring of trees, at 783 feet, can be seen for miles around, both to the south and the north. There was a Roman Camp here in the 3rd and 4th centuries.

RESTAURANTS
Georges Carvery
Tel: (0903) 892947
Old Smithy Restaurant
Tel: (0903) 892271

PUBLIC HOUSE
The Franklands Arms
Old London Road. Tel: (0903) 892220

OTHER AMENITY
GARDEN CENTRE
English Water Gardens
Rock Lane . Tel: (0903) 892006

🐦 🐦 🐦 🐦 🐦 🐦 🐦

WEST ASHLING

Slightly south of East Ashling, there are some some pretty cottages, some thatched, some flint, and a duck pond.

PUBLIC HOUSE
The Richmond Arms
Mill Lane. Tel: (0243) 575730

WEST DEAN HOUSE

WEST CHILTINGTON

A prosperous village to the east of Pulborough in the Weald, divided into two parts. The original group is around the crossroads, and to the south at the Common are expensive modern houses. Outside the Norman church the old stocks are still to be seen. Half a mile to the west is a smock windmill of c.1800.
Population: 2,042.

HOTEL

The Roundabout Hotel
Monkmead Lane. Tel: (079 83) 3838

PUBLIC HOUSES

Elephant & Castle
Church Street. Tel: (079 83) 3307
The Five Bells
Smock Alley . Tel: (079 83) 2143
Queen's Head
The Hollow. Tel: (079 83) 3143
The Rising Sun
Street, Nutbourne.Tel: (079 83) 2191

🐾 🐾 🐾 🐾 🐾 🐾 🐾

WEST DEAN

A downland village set in the leafy Lavant valley close to Goodwood. Flint predominates; flint cot-

tages and flint walls, a flint church, St Andrew, parts of which date back to before the Norman Conquest. West Dean College, built in Gothic style, is also made of flint. It holds courses in traditional country crafts.
Population: 424.

PLACES OF INTEREST

West Dean House

RESTAURANT

Trundle Inn
Tel: (024 363) 246

OTHER AMENITY

GARDEN CENTRE
West Dean Estate (Edward James Foundation)
West Dean Gardens, Applehouse Nursery. Tel: (024 363) 205

🐾 🐾 🐾 🐾 🐾 🐾 🐾

WEST HOATHLY

West Hoathly is south-east of Crawley close to the East Sussex border. St Margaret's is a simple Norman church, and round about there are several large manor houses of historic note.
Population: 2,133.

87

WEST WITTERING CHURCH, OF SAXON ORIGINS

WEST WITTERING

A wealthy village on the Selsey peninsular. West Wittering is the 'posh' one of the two Witterings, with some beautifully restored cottages, and lots of trees. The walls are made of flint or rounded pebbles from the beach. There are expensive houses rather than seaside bungalows, and consequently there is a more permanent population than in East Wittering. The church is a mixture of styles, with Saxon origins.
Population: 2,598.

PLACES OF INTEREST
Priest House
Tel: (0342) 810479
Months Open: March 25 - October 31. Days Open: Daily, except Tuesday. Hours Open: 11am-5.30pm, Sunday 2-5.30pm. Admission: £1. Children 50p.

PUBLIC HOUSE
The Cat Inn
North Lane. Tel: (0342) 810369

🐾 🐾 🐾 🐾 🐾 🐾 🐾

WEST LAVINGTON

A church and a few large houses make up this settlement south-east of Midhurst; a delightful rural suburb. Richard Cobden, who believed in Free Trade and led the Anti-Corn-Law League (1838-46), lived at Dunford House, now owned by the YMCA. A sandstone obelisk in the village states his principles concisely: Free Trade, Peace, Goodwill among Nations.
Population: 392.

PUBLIC HOUSE
The Royal Oak
Chichester Road. Tel: (073 081) 4611

🐾 🐾 🐾 🐾 🐾 🐾 🐾

WEST MARDEN

A very cosy village in this totally unspoilt and beautiful part of the county. West Marden is the biggest of the Mardens, and its flint cottages are built on a hillside on the road between Emsworth and South Harting.

PUBLIC HOUSE
Victoria Inn
Tel: (0705) 631330

RESTAURANT
The Spinning Wheel
77 Rookwood Road. Tel: (0243) 513507

PUBLIC HOUSES
The Lamb Inn
Chichester Road. Tel: (0243) 511105
Old House at Home
Cakeham Road. Tel: (0243) 511234

OTHER AMENITIES
BUS & COACH SERVICES
Westrings Coaches
48 Marine Drive West. Tel: (0243) 672411

CARAVAN PARKS
Walnut Tree Caravan Park
Island Meadow, Chapel Lane. Tel: (0243) 513084
Wicks Farm Caravan Park
Redlands Lane. PO20 8QD Tel: (0243) 513116

GARDEN CENTRE
Bramber Nursery
Chichester Road. Tel: (0243) 512004

WATER SPORTS
Dee Caldwell
West Wittering Car Park, West Strand. Tel: (0243) 513077

🐾 🐾 🐾 🐾 🐾 🐾 🐾

WESTERGATE

A village north of Bognor Regis stretched along the main road, that has experienced quite extensive bungalow-building in recent years. One or two old flint cottages are scattered amongst the new housing.

RESTAURANT
Starters Restaurant
Tel: (024 368) 3092

PUBLIC HOUSES

The Labour in Vain
Nyton Road. Tel: (0243) 543173

The Old Stable
Westergate Street. Tel: (0243) 543092

OTHER AMENITIES

CAR HIRE/CHAUFFEUR DRIVE
Crown Chauffeur Service
11 Elm Road. Tel: (0243) 542695

LEISURE CENTRE
Aldingbourne Community Centre
Olivers Meadow, Westergate Street. Tel: (0243) 543948

🐾 🐾 🐾 🐾 🐾 🐾 🐾

WESTHAMPNETT

A hamlet on Stane Street one mile out of Chichester. The old schoolroom standing at a crossroads must be one of the smallest in the country.
Population: 450.

HOTEL
Chichester Resort Hotel
Tel: (0243) 786351

OTHER AMENITY
CARAVAN PARK
Southern Leisure Lakeside Village
Vinnetrow Road. Tel: (0243) 787715

🐾 🐾 🐾 🐾 🐾 🐾 🐾

WICK

Essentially part of Littlehampton, Wick is just to the north, and its main claim to fame currently is being the headquarters of the Body Shop.

HOTEL
The Dew Drop Inn
96, Wick Street. Tel: (0903) 716459

RESTAURANTS
Blue Gingham
6 Wick Parade, Wick Street. Tel: (0903) 721054
Candlewick Spread
80, Wick Street. Tel: (0903) 730756

PUBLIC HOUSES
Six Bells
Lyminster Road. Tel: (0903) 713639
True Blue Inn
79, Wick Street.Tel: (0903) 713615

OTHER AMENITIES

CAR HIRE
Altar
6, True Blue Precinct. Tel: (0903) 716171/726622

CARAVAN PARKS
Caravan Club
Summer Side, Worthing Road. Tel: (0903) 714240
White Rose Touring Park
Mill Lane. Tel: (0903) 716176

GARDEN CENTRES
Foxdale Nursery
Toddington Lane. Tel: (0903) 715688
R.F. Molica
Old Mead House, Old Mead Road. Tel: (0903) 713567
Old Mead Nursery
Marina House, Old Mead Road. Tel: (0903) 715981

TAXI
Chauffeur Taxis
135a Wick Street. Tel: (0903) 715117

PUBLIC HOUSE
Royal Oak
Wineham Lane. Tel: (0444) 881252

🐾 🐾 🐾 🐾 🐾 🐾 🐾

WISBOROUGH GREEN

A quintessential Wealden village located in glorious countryside between Billingshurst and Petworth, that is indeed green, being mainly centred around a huge rectangular green, with village life on all sides. Half-timbered, tile-hung and weatherboard houses and shops, and horse-chestnut trees line three sides of the green, and to the north, majestic oaks grow in parkland. In one corner there is an inviting rustic-looking pub, in another the 11th century church. In the Middle Ages the church attracted many pilgrims, purporting to contain sacred relics, including St James' hair-shirt and bones. On a summer's weekend cricket is usually being played on the green, and the whole atmosphere is as typical Sussex village as is imaginable, and a must for visitors from abroad.
Population: 1,326.

HOTEL
The Cricketers Arms
The Green. Tel: (0403) 700369

GUEST HOUSE
D.C. Mitchell
The Old Wharf. Tel: (040 381) 4096

PUBLIC HOUSE
Three Crowns
Billingshurst Road. Tel: (0403) 700207

OTHER AMENITY
GARDEN CENTRE
Idehurst Fuchsia Nursery
Strood Green. Tel: (0403) 700736

🐦 🐦 🐦 🐦 🐦 🐦 🐦

WIVELSFIELD GREEN
A little Wealden village east of Burgess Hill.

PUBLIC HOUSE
The Royal Oak Inn
Jacobs Post, Ditching Common. RH15 OSJ
Tel: (044 484) 263

🐦 🐦 🐦 🐦 🐦 🐦 🐦

WOODGATE
Most remarkable for its level crossing. On the northern approach to Bognor Regis.

PUBLIC HOUSE
The Prince of Wales
Lidsey Road. Tel: (0243) 543247

OTHER AMENITY
CARAVAN PARK
Willows Caravan Park
Lidsey Road. Tel: (0243) 543124

🐦 🐦 🐦 🐦 🐦 🐦 🐦

WOODMANCOTE
A tiny rural village with a pleasant pub in farming country north-west of Chichester.
Population: 434.

PUBLIC HOUSE
Woodmancote Arms
Tel: (0243) 372612

OTHER AMENITY
CAR HIRE/CHAUFFEUR DRIVE
Exec-Cars
Ffynon, South Lane. Tel: (0243) 372862

WOOLBEDING
A picturesque ancient manor set in delightful countryside, west of Midhurst.
Population: 158.

🐦 🐦 🐦 🐦 🐦 🐦 🐦

WORTH
Immediately south of suburban Crawley, and on the edge of quite extensive woodland (and not far from the M23), this village boasts a solid Saxon church.
Population: 13,160.

HOTEL
Wentworth Lodge Hotel
Turners Hill Road. Tel: (0293) 884806

OTHER AMENITIES
CAR HIRE
Thrifty Car Rental
Wentworth Lodge Hotel. Tel: (0293) 886438
Vintage Wedding Hire
The Barn, Caxtons, Turners Hill Road. Tel: (0293) 886488

GARDEN CENTRE
G.R. Wiltshire
Northside Balcombe Road. Tel: (0293) 884287

🐦 🐦 🐦 🐦 🐦 🐦 🐦

WORTHING
Worthing shares a similar pedigree with many coastal resorts, being a small fishing village until it was turned into a fashionable watering hole during the late 18th century, when the 'craze' began after Brighton's success. The Royal patronage came from George III, and there remain some elegant Georgian terraces as testimony. But there are few other buildings of great interest, and Worthing has latterly found fame of sorts by having the oldest average population in the country.

PLACES OF INTEREST
Highdown Hill
National Trust site of ancient cemeteries.
Worthing Museum & Art Gallery
Town Hall, Chapel Road.
Tel: (0903) 39999
Archaeology of Worthing region; toys and dolls, English costume, ceramics, glass, paintings, exhibition programme.
Months Open: All year. Days Open: Monday to Saturday. Hours Open: 10am-6pm April to September, 10am-5pm October to March. Bank Holidays: Open except New Year's Day,

CHANCTONBURY RING, THE DOWNS NORTH OF WORTHING (PAGE 86)

Good Friday, Christmas & Boxing Day. Admission: Free. Easy access for disabled.

HOTELS

Ainslea Court Hotel
Abbey Road. Tel: (0903) 30442

The Anchorage Hotel
169 Brighton Road. Tel: (0903) 38535

Ardington Hotel
Steyne Gardens. Tel: (0903) 30451

The Beach Hotel
Marine Parade. Tel: (0903) 340001

Beechwood Hall Hotel
Park Crescent. Tel: (0903) 32872
BEDROOMS: 8 Single, (8 en suite, 8 TV, 8 phone, 8 tea/coffee)
B&B £ 32.00. 4 Double, (4 en suite, 4 TV, 4 phone, 4 tea/coffee)
B&B £ 45.00. 5 Twin, (5 en suite, 5 TV, 5 phone, 5 tea/coffee)
B&B £ 45.00. 1 Family, (1 en suite, 1 TV, 1 phone, 1 tea/coffee)
£ 50.00. HOTEL INFORMATION: CF. W. B. F. 60 space Car Park. Dogs. Credit Cards: Ac. Am.
Weekend Breaks: 2 nights: £ 48.00. 3 nights: £ 72.00. Allowance towards dinner: £ 8.50.

Belmont Private Hotel
211 Brighton Road. Tel: (0903) 202678

Berkeley Hotel
Marine Parade. Tel: (0903) 820000

Berys Hotel
4 Park Crescent. Tel: (0903) 31365

Blenheim Hotel
23 Thorn Road. Tel: (0903) 33095

The Burlington Hotel
Marine Parade. Tel: (0903) 211222

The Cavandish Hotel
Marine Parade. Tel: (0903) 36767

Chapmans Hotel
27, Railway Approach. Tel: (0903) 30690

Chatsworth Hotel
The Steyne. Tel: (0903) 36103

The Cumberland Hotel
Marine Parade. Tel: (0903) 35084

The Delmar Hotel
2, New Parade. Tel: (0903) 211834

Downlands Beefeater Steak House
Upper Brighton Road. Tel: (0903) 34085

91

Duneim Private Hotel
5, New Parade. Tel: (0903) 36536

Eardley Hotel
Marine Parade. Tel: (0903) 34444

Garendon Hotel
1 - 5, Navarino Road. Tel: (0903) 35693

Granville Hotel
74, Marine Parade. Tel: (0903) 39464

Heene House Hotel
140, Heene Road. BN11 4PJ. Tel: (0903) 33213

Henry House
189, Heene Road. Tel: (0903) 32875

Holcombe Hotel
92, Heene Road. Tel: (0903) 32027

Ingleside Hotel
155/165, Brighton Road. Tel: (0903) 203215

Kingsway Hotel
117/119, Marine Parade. Tel: (0903) 37542

The Langham Hotel
121, Marine Parade. Tel: (0903) 200363

The Lantern Hotel
54, Shelley Road. Tel: (0903) 38476

The Lennox Hotel
Chapel Road. Tel: (0903) 37001

The Marine Plaza Hotel
36/39, Marine Parade. Tel: (0903) 32078

Marine View Hotel
111, Marine Parade. Tel: (0903) 38413

Mayfair Hotel
11 / 12, Heene Terrace. Tel: (0903) 201943

Moorings Private Hotel
4, Selden Road. Tel: (0903) 208882

New Eversley Hotel
121, Brighton Road. Tel: (0903) 39827

Park House Hotel
4, St Georges Road. Tel: (0903) 207939

The Royal Oak Inn
67, Brighton Road. Tel: (0903) 38888

The Shelley Hotel
15, Shelley Road. Tel: (0903) 38521

St Georges Lodge Hotel
46, Chesswood Road. Tel: (0903) 208926

Sussex Hotel
12, Queens Road. Tel: (0903) 33270

Touchstones Hotel
11, Shakespeare Road. Tel: (0903) 36023

Villa Marianela
5, Windsor Road. Tel: (0903) 210265

Warwick House Hotel
11, Warwick Gardens. Tel: (0903) 35488

The Westbrook Hotel
5, Westbrook. Tel: (0903) 25217

Windsor House Hotel
14-20, Windsor Road. Tel: (0903) 39655

Wolsey Hotel
181, Brighton Road. Tel: (0903) 34255

GUEST HOUSES

The Ashlee Guest House
22, Church Walk. Tel: (0903) 30080

Avon Lodge Guest House
5, Chaucer Road. Tel: (0903) 30810

The Beacons
18, Shelley Road. Tel: (0903) 30948

Belvadere Guest House
12, Windsor Road. Tel: (0903) 202949

Blair Guest House
11, St. George Street. Tel: (0903) 34071
Months Open: All year. Number of Bedrooms: 7. (6 with
bathroom). B&B per person: £15. TV in rooms. Evening meals
Car Park: 3 spaces. Proprietors: Mr & Mrs M.D. Taylor.

Burcott Guest House
6, Windsor Road. Tel: (0903) 35163

Christian Alliance of Women & Girls
5, Byron Road. Tel: (0903) 36639

Delamere Guest House
9, Oxford Road. Tel: (0903) 37128

Dowell A.E.G. Wayside Guest House
Wyke Avenue. Tel: (0903) 39615

Edelweiss Guest House
50, Alexandra Road. Tel: (0903) 36988

Emelba Guest House
46, Alexandra Road. Tel: (0903) 31058

Glenill Guest House
21, Alexandra Road. Tel: (0903) 202756

Helena House
33, St. Georges Road. Tel: (0903) 32287

High Beach Guest House
201, Brighton Road. Tel: (0903) 36389

High Trees Guest House
2, Warwick Gardens . Tel: (0903) 36668

Kinross Guest House
7, Alexandra Road. Tel: (0903) 207030

Manor Guest House
100, Broadwater Road. Tel: (0903) 36028

Marina Guest House
191, Brighton Road. Tel: (0903) 207844

Meldrum Guest House
8, Windsor Road. Tel: (0903) 33808

Merlin Guest House
22, Wordsworth Road. Tel: (0903) 38362

Merton Guest House
96, Broadwater Road. Tel: (0903) 38222

Oakville Guest House
13, Wyke Avenue. Tel: (0903) 205026

Olinda Guest House
199, Brighton Road. Tel: (0903) 206114

Penland Guest House

194, Heene Road. Tel: (0903) 211763
Queens Lodge
20, Queens Road. Tel: (0903) 31035
Sans Souci
35, Alexandra Road. Tel: (0903) 36556
Sea Spray
195, Brighton Road. Tel: (0903) 33635
St. Mary Convent Guest House
14, Westbrooke. Tel: (0903) 33530
Warwick Guest House
29, Warwick Road. Tel: (0903) 35865
Williton Guest House
10, Windsor Road. Tel: (0903) 37974
Woodland Guest House
20, Warwick Gardens. Tel: (0903) 33557
Wynchcroft Guest House
10, Wordsworth Road. Tel: (0903) 34192

RESTAURANTS

A Great Meal
Tel: (0903) 32982
Anurag Indian Restaurant
121, Rectory Road. Tel: (0903) 66384
Athenian Restaurant
41, Brighton Road. Tel: (0903) 210737
The Bowl Inn Restaurant
Tel: (0903) 37722
Cafe Continental
17, Warwick Street. Tel: (0903) 32920
Cameo Restaurant
5, Bath Place. Tel: (0903) 38864
Carriages
36, South Farm Road. Tel: (0903) 820642
Central Park Restaurant
44, Portland Road. Tel: (0903) 201664
Chalet Restaurant
5, Crescent Road. Tel: (0903) 36480
Chompers
2, Colonade Street. Tel: (0903) 30248
Connaught Corner House Restaurant
32, Marine Parade. Tel: (0903) 210084
The Covent Garden Carvery
16, Windsor Road. Tel: (0903) 39655
Curryland
239, Tarring Road. Tel: (0903) 504631
Domingos Restaurant
12, Montague Place. Tel: (0903) 821393
Fogarty's Restaurant
10, Prospect Place. Tel: (0903) 212984
Frooms Regency Restaurant
7, Brunswick Road. Tel: (0903) 820605
The Golden Bengal
40, Lyndhurst Road. Tel: (0903) 208730
Golden City

11a, Goring Road. Tel: (0903) 44992
Goodwins
19a, Goring Road. Tel: (0903) 502845
Grapes Bistro
3a, Bath Place. Tel: (0903) 32424
The Greek Taverna Restaurant
46, Chesswood Road. Tel: (0903) 37712
Guildbourne Lounge
Unit 11, Guildbourne Centre. Tel: (0903) 206691
Highdown Thai Cuisine
Tel: (0903) 506792
Hong Kong Chef
205, Tarring Road. Tel: (0903) 37717
Intimate Steak Bar
5 - 6, Plaza Parade. Tel: (0903) 36053
Josephs Licensed Restaurant
76, Brighton Road. Tel: (0903) 39477
La Difference Restaurant
12, Crescent Road. Tel: (0903) 205370
La Terrazza Restaurant
15, Bedford Row. Tel: (0903) 209314
Laings Restaurant
3, The Arcade. Tel: (0903) 211064
Le Gourmet
37, Rowlands Road. Tel: (0903) 211338
The Little Mill Restaurant
177, Tarring Road. Tel: (0903) 36654
Lockwoods Restaurant
53, Rowlands Road. Tel: (0903) 37534
Lucky House chinese Restaurant
75, Chapel Road. Tel: (0903) 36654
Macmillans
38, Ann Street. Tel: (0903) 200688
The Mahaan Tandoori Restaurant
181, Montague Street. Tel: (0903) 205449
McDonalds
10, Liverpool Road. Tel: (0903) 212410
The Mississippi
187, Montague Street. Tel: (0903) 39712
Mr Pastry
8, Warwick Lane. Tel: (0903) 212780
Mrs Beeton's Restaurant
7, Station Parade. Tel: (0903) 48465
The New Dynasty Chinese Restaurant
49, Brighton Road. Tel: (0903) 30209
Paragon Restaurant
10, Brunswick Road. Tel: (0903) 33367
The Peking Restaurant
88, Ham Road. Tel: (0903) 39226
Peppers Restaurant
171, Findon Road. Tel: (0903) 873385
Pizza Express
Stanford Square, 20-22 Warwick Street. BN11 3DJ
Tel: (0903) 821133

The Pizza Hut
8, South Street. Tel: (0903) 30494

Pizzeria La Cantina
18b, Warwick Street. Tel: (0903) 36860

The Platter
14, Teville Gate. Tel: (0903) 205093

Portlands Restaurant
75, Portland Road. Tel: (0903) 31242

Raffles
2, Caledonian Place. Tel: (0903) 210066

Rendezvous Cafe
21, Marine Parade. Tel: (0903) 200823

The River Kwai Restaurant
16, Ambrose Place. Tel: (0903) 211901

Sama Santa Restaurant
Highdown House, Littlehampton Road. Tel: (0903) 503774

Saqui
30 - 31, Marine Parade. Tel: (0903) 820783/39104

Sarahs Restaurant
7, Montague Street. Tel: (0903) 483738

Shades Of Elegance Restaurant
72, Marine Parade. Tel: (0903) 36414

Shahi Tandoori Restaurant
35, Brighton Road. Tel: (0903) 205685

Shajan Tandoori Restaurant
54, Broadwater Road. Tel: (0903) 213480

Shalimar Tandoori
16a, Portland Market. Tel: (0903) 39675

Sri-Nager Indian Restaurant
66, Teville Road. Tel: (0903) 30638

Steers
Marine Parade. Tel: (0903) 32982

Sunny Restaurant
58, Ham Road. Tel: (0903) 30061

The Sussex Kitchen Restaurant
20, Warwick Road. Tel: (0903) 202335

The Tajmahal
34, Brighton Road. Tel: (0903) 31233

Thomas A Beckett
146, Rectory Road. Tel: (0903) 66643

Toby Jug Restaurant
40, High Street. Tel: (0903) 211012

Trenchers Restaurant
118/120, Portland Road. BN11 1QA Tel: (0903) 820287

York Restaurant
23 Victoria Buildings , Brighton Road. Tel: (0903) 211185

PUBLIC HOUSES

Alexandra Hotel
28, Lyndhurst Road.Tel: (0903) 34833

Beachcomber
New Street. Tel: (0903) 36646

The Bear Inn
17, Market Place.Tel: (0903) 30777

The Boat And Anchor
42, Marine Parade.Tel: (0903) 32538

The Castle Inn
1, Newland Road.Tel: (0903) 30816

Chapmans Wine Lodge
80/82, Marine Parade.Tel: (0903) 33825

Cinque Port
Tarring Road. Tel: (0903) 39527

Clifton Arms
Tarring Road. Tel: (0903) 39527

Cobden Arms
Cobden Road. Tel: (0903) 36856

Cricketers
Broadway Green. Tel: (0903) 33369

The Dolphin Hotel
Dominion Road. Tel: (0903) 33667

The Egremont
32 Brighton Road. Tel: (0903) 201541

The Elms
66, Brodwater Street.Tel: (0903) 34130

The Fountain
20, Chapel Road.Tel: (0903) 204255

Globe Inn
Newland Road. Tel: (0903) 33797

The Half Brick
Brighton Road. Tel: (0903) 34196

The Inn On The Prom
18, Marine Parade.Tel: (0903) 35387

J.B.'s Bar
New Street. Tel: (0903) 821530

John Selden Hotel
Salvington Road. Tel: (0903) 64986

The Jolly Brewer
Clifton Road. Tel: (0903) 20006

The Lamb Inn
Salvington Road. Tel: (0903) 63356

Marine Parade Bar
20, Marine Parade.Tel: (0903) 201663

The Montague Arms
149, Montague Street.Tel: (0903) 202414

The Norfolk Hotel
Chapel Road . Tel: (0903) 38504

North Star
Littlehampton Road. Tel: (0903) 44913

The Old House At Home
Broadwater Street . Tel: (0903) 32661

Pawn & Castle
21, Rowland Road.Tel: (0903) 36232

The Prom
18, Marine Parade.Tel: (0903) 35387

Rose & Crown
169-173, Montague Street.Tel: (0903) 20623

Selden Arms
41, Lyndhurst Road.Tel: (0903) 34854

The Southdown Public House
North Court Road. Tel: (0903) 33307

Strollers
56, Heene Road.Tel: (0903) 30355

The Broadwater
4 Broadwater Street West. Tel: (0903) 38675

The Thieves Kitchen
10, Warwick Street.Tel: (0903) 37978

Tiroler Bar
31, Guilbourne Centre.Tel: (0903) 207334

Warwick Arms
25, Warwick Street.Tel: (0903) 206088

Wheatsheaf
Richmond Road. Tel: (0903) 207395

The Wine Lodge
80/82, Marine Parade.Tel: (0903) 33825

CAFES & TEA ROOMS

Brougham Cafe
12, Brougham Road. Tel: (0903) 202817

Brownies
10 Dowlands Parade, Upper Brighton Road. Tel: (0903) 32114

Cabana Cafe & Kiosks
Beach Hole Grounds, East Promenade. Tel: (0903) 32667

The Coffee House
3 Liverpool Buildings , Liverpool Road. Tel: (0903) 201074

Dayvilles Ice Cream
13, Warwick Street. Tel: (0903) 208411

The Highway Cafe
80, Brighton Road. Tel: (0903) 38670

Kosla W.
30, Railway Approach. Tel: (0903) 208470

Kwick Snak
11 Portland Market , Portland Road. Tel: (0903) 33006

Lido Snack Bar
Marine Parade. Tel: (0903) 35675

Lingalong Cafe
164, Findon Road. Tel: (0903) 64092

Mabel's Muncher
Station Parade, Tarring Road. Tel: (0903) 504740

Macari's Ice Cream Parlour
24, Marine Parade. Tel: (0903) 39543

Meggies
28, Marine Parade. Tel: (0903) 39300

Tati Cafe & Patisserie
6 Stanford Square , Warwick Street. Tel: (0903) 207060

Teville Diner & Take Away
32, Teville Road. Tel: (0903) 38023

Thingummys Cafe
32, Broadwater Road. Tel: (0903) 212723

Vittles Cafe
29, West Buildings. Tel: (0903) 202310

OTHER AMENITIES

ART GALLERIES

Terrace Gallery
7 Liverpool Terrace. Tel: (0903) 212926

Viewpoint Gallery
5 Stanford Square, Warwick Street. Tel: (0903) 205863

BUS & COACH SERVICES

Cedarbus
20, Neville Gate. Tel: (0903) 214321

Southdown Motor Services
23, Marine Parade. Tel: (0903) 37661/205587

Sussex Leamland
2 Arcade Buildings, South Street . Tel: (0903) 212188

CAR HIRE

Ace Car Hire
34, Railway Approach. Tel: (0903) 34220

Ballam's Of Sussex
11 - 17, Alfred Place. Tel: (0903) 35769

Bridal & Business Cars
5, Douglas Close. Tel: (0903) 504148

Bridal Car Hire
10, Westbrooke. Tel: (0903) 35869

Bridal Carriage Co.
Sky Ways , Chalet Road. Tel: (0903) 503671

Broadwater Car Hire
18, Northbrook Road. Tel: (0903) 212820/35000

Caffyns
Broadwater Road. Tel: (0903) 31111

Carousel Cars
38, Coleridge Crescent. Tel: (0903) 503060

Gem Private Hire
43a, Taring Road. Tel: (0903) 504481/212281

H. D. Steele & Son
Teville Road. Tel: (0903) 37527

J. R. Cars
77, Portland Road. Tel: (0903) 212000

J.D.T.
Basfords Lane . Tel: (0903) 31606

Moore's Of Worthing
7, Heene Place. Tel: (0903) 202250

Orme Road Rentals
Orme Road Garage , Orme Road . Tel: (0903) 38147

Pavilion Car Hire
122, Becket Road. Tel: (0903) 820800

Premier-Abbey Cars
33A, Rowlands Road. Tel: (0903) 204225/6

Zed Cars
90a, Brighton Road. Tel: (0903) 212282

CARAVAN PARK

Caravan Club Ltd.

Northbrook Farm. Tel: (0903) 502962

CINEMA
The Dome Cinema
Marine Parade. Tel: (0903) 200461

GARDEN CENTRES
Broadwater Conservatory
33, Upper Brighton Road. Tel: (0903) 30925
Handcross Garden Centre
Littlehampton Road. Tel: (0903) 42003

NIGHT CLUB
Bubbles Club
31, Chatsworth Road. Tel: (0903) 211926

SNOOKER CENTRES
Connaught Club
Connaught House, 32-34 Marine Parade. Tel: (0903) 214636
Zan's Billiard Hall
12, Bath Place. Tel: (0903) 38744

STORES
Bentalls
South Street. Tel: (0903) 31801
BHS
56, Montague Street. Tel: (0903) 35135
Debenhams Plc.
14/20, South Street. Tel: (0903) 34321/31733
Marks & Spencer Plc.
51, Montague Street. Tel: (0903) 212381
Woolworths
35, Montague Street. Tel: (0903) 201237

TAXIS
A & A Taxis
16, Highdown Avenue. Tel: (0903) 67932
Arrow
27/33, Lyndhurst Road. Tel: (0903) 204378
Austin Hire Taxis
34, Railway Approach. BN11 1UR Tel: (0903) 36334
A. Brown
65, Victoria Road. Tel: (0903) 205566
D.J. Taxis
51, Mansfield Road. Tel: (0903) 210074
Dial A Car
29, Horrow Road. Tel: (0903) 201790
Roller Cars
43a, New Broadway. Tel: (0903) 30881
Star Cars
2 Portland Depot, Bridge Road. Tel: (0903) 68957
Target Private Hire
43a New Broadway, Tarring Road. Tel: (0903) 32350

Taxi-Cab Rank
Town Centre, Chapel Road. Tel: (0903) 30302
Wortax
65, Victoria Road. Tel: (0903) 35532
Worthing Central Taxi Service
Railway Approach. Tel: (0903) 200619

THEATRES
Connaught Theatre
Union Place. BN11 1LG Tel: (0903) 35333
The Worthing Pavilion & Assembly Hall
Marine Parade. Tel: (0903) 820500
Theatre & Concert Halls
Months Open: All year round. Days Open: Summer nightly. Other times as advertised. Hours Open: 7.45pm summer, 8pm other times unless advertised. Bank Holidays: As advertised. Full summer season of nightly entertainment. Regular star concerts throughout the year. Regular children's entertainment in school holidays. Christmas Circus Spectacular. In addition to variety entertainment, wrestling, country music, talent shows, organ and classical music, ballroom dancing etc. There are also exhibitions and conferences.Rates: As advertised. Manager: Mr P Bailey.

🐾 🐾 🐾 🐾 🐾 🐾 🐾

YAPTON

A scattered village, with no central group, but with one or two nice cottages, and a pub that features in the Guinness Book of Records for having the longest name, 'The Shoulder of Mutton and Cucumbers Inn', which weighs in with 34 letters.
Population: 3,735.

PUBLIC HOUSES
The Black Dog
North End Road. Tel: (0243) 551310
The Lamb Inn
Bilsham Road. Tel: (0243) 551232
The Maypole Inn
Maypole Lane. Tel: (0243) 551417
Shoulder of Mutton & Cucumbers Inn
Burndell Road. Tel: (0243) 551429

OTHER AMENITIES
GARDEN CENTRE
Regal Wire Products
Downside, Main Road. BN18 0EY Tel: (0243) 553173

TAXI
Barnham Station Cars
24 Canal Road. Tel: (0243) 551753

🐾 🐾 🐾 🐾 🐾 🐾 🐾

BOSHAM HARBOUR

AFK: A.F. Kirsting. PP&P: Portsmouth Publishing & Printing. NT: National Trust.

CHANCTONBURY RING (SEE PAGE 86)

INDEX OF AMENITIES

Name	Town	Town Page Number
Denmans Ltd Plant Centre	Fontwell	44
Handcross Garden Centre	Handcross	47
Allwood Bros	Hassocks	48
E. G. Budd & Son	Hassocks	48
Eatwoods Nurseries	Hassocks	48
Straffords Garden centre	Hassocks	48
D. J. Shepherd	Haywards heath	48
Westlands	Henfield	50
Woodside Farm	Hookwood	50
Hillier Garden Centre	Horsham	50
Mill Lane Nursery	Littlehampton	57
Ockendens	Littlehampton	57
Howards Nursery Centre	Lower Beeding	59
Country Gardens at Chichester	Merston	60
Southgate Nursery	North Mundham	63
Nutbourne Nurseries	Nutbourne	64
Murrells Garden Centre	Pulborough	68
Nightingales Garden Centre	Pullborough	68
Freshacres Nurseries	Runcton	69
Hill Brothers	Runcton	69
Manor Nurseries	Runcton	69
Combes	Rustington	69
Lowertrees Plant centre	Rustington	69
Scaynes Hill Nursery	Scaynes Hill	70
B. T. Edmonds	Shoreham-by-Sea	72
Sandel Perkins	Shoreham-by-Sea	72
Shoreham Garden Shop	Shoreham-by-Sea	72
Rotherhill Nursery	Stedham	81
Aylings of Trotton	Trotton	85
de Vries	Walberton	85
Yeomans Nurseries	Warningcamp	86
English Water Gardens	Washington	86
Gubbins	West Chiltington	87
West Dean Gardens	West Dean	87
Bramber Nursery	West Wittering	88
Foxdale Nursery	Wick	89
Molica	Wick	89
Old Mead Nursery	Wick	89
Perella P.	Wick	89
Idehurst Fuchsia Nursery	Wisborough Green	89
Wiltshire	Worth	90
Broadwater Conservatory	Worthing	90
Handcross Garden Centre	Worthing	90
Regal Wire Products	Yapton	90

HEALTH CLUBS

Name	Town	Town Page Number
Coconut	Billingshurst	13
Allington Health Club	Crawley	31
Body Shop	Horsham	50
Horsham Diet Centre	Horsham	50
Tip Top Health Club	Horsham	50
Dimension Health & Fitness Centre	Littlehampton	57
Brighton Sun Club	Scaynes Hill	70
Weight Watchers Ltd.	Worthing	90

HEALTH CLUBS & CENTRES

Name	Town	Town Page Number
Images	Bognor Regis	15
Body Sense Chichester	Chichester	24
Profiles	Chichester	24

HOLIDAY CAMPS

Name	Town	Town Page Number
South Coast World	Bognor Regis	15
Sussex Beach Holiday Village	Earnley	35
Sussex Coast	Middleton-on-Sea	60
Little Spain Holiday Homes	Selsey	70

LEISURE CENTRES

Name	Town	Town Page Number
Broadbridge Heath Sports Centre	Broadbridge Heath	22
Martlets Hall	Burgess Hill	22
Sheddingdean Community Centre	Burgess Hill	22
Sidney West Centre	Burgess Hill	22
Swimming Centre	Burgess Hill	22
Westgate Leisure Centre	Chichester	24
Bewbush Neighbourhood Centre	Crawley	31
Crawley Leisure Centre	Crawley	31
Kings Centre	East Grinstead	36
Arun Leisure Centre	Felpham	41
Clair Hall	Haywards Heath	48
Dolphin Leisure Centre	Haywards Heath	48
Lancing Manor Leisure Centre	Lancing	55
Grange Centre	Midhurst	61
Aldingbourne Community Centre	Westergate	88
Durrington Community Centre	Worthing	90

MARINAS

Name	Town	Town Page Number
Chichester Yacht Basin	Birdham	14
St. Georges Marina	Chichester	24
Thornham Marina	Prinsted	67

NIGHT CLUBS

Name	Town	Town Page Number
Bentley's Nightclub	Bognor Regis	15
Sheiks Nightclub & Disco	Bognor Regis	15
Toppers Night Club	Bognor Regis	15
Martines Night Club	East Grinstead	36
Champagne Night Club	Horsham	50
Spencers	Hurstpierpoint	53
Keystones	Lancing	55
Bubbles Club	Worthing	90

SAUNAS & SOLARIA

Name	Town	Town Page Number
Dial-a-Tan	Bognor Regis	15
Reelaks	Bognor Regis	15
Sun Dial Leisure Services	Crawley	31
Sussex Tan	Ford	44
Sussex Tan	Middleton-on-Sea	60
Trinline Health Clinic	Worthing	90

SNOOKER CENTRES

Name	Town	Town Page Number
Chichester Snooker Club	Chichester	24
Triangle Club	Chichester	24
Dunnings Mill Snooker Club	East Grinstead	36
Green Baize Billiards & Snooker Centre	Horsham	50
Tower Snooker Club	Littlehampton	57
Connaught Club	Worthing	90
Zan's Billiard Hall	Worthing	90

STORES

Name	Town	Town Page Number
FJ Bobby of Bognor	Bognor Regis	15
Marks & Spencer plc	Bognor Regis	15
Reynolds & Co. (Furnishers)	Bognor Regis	15
Army & Navy	Chichester	24
Hoopers	Chichester	24
Marks & Spencer plc	Chichester	24
Alders International	Crawley	31
Co-Operative Retail Services	Crawley	31
Littlewoods Organisation Plc	Crawley	31
Marks & Spencer Plc.	Crawley	31
Woolworths Plc	Crawley	31
Woolworths plc	Crawley	31
Woolworths plc	East Grinstead	36
W.H. Smith & Son	Haywards Heath	48
Woolworths Plc	Haywards Heath	48
Chart & Lawrence	Horsham	50
Marks & Spencer plc	Horsham	50
Woolworths	Lancing	55
Woolworths	Littlehampton	57
Woolworths	Poynings	67
Woolworths	Rustington	69
East Street Arcade Ltd	Shoreham-by-Sea	72
Woolworths	Shoreham-by-Sea	72
Bentalls	Worthing	90
BHS	Worthing	90
Debenhams Plc.	Worthing	90

In the compilation of this guide, it is inevitable that there will be errors, omissions, duplications, and wrong dialling codes, although we have made every effort to eliminate them. In the most part this due to the march of time, restaurants close, or change their names, and although we did send every establishment listed a form that they could check and if necessary amend the data, not everyone returned the form. The information in italics listed below certain establishments has been supplied by themselves, and should be accurate.

It is our stated intention to create as accurate a database, and therefore guide book, as possible, and in this pursuit we would invite readers and contributors to send in details of omissions or incorrect listings on the form below (please photocopy it and return it to us). We would also be most interested in any editorial corrections or additions, any fact or legend associated with anywhere listed.

Please Photocopy the form, complete and return it to:
Gaymer's Guides, 24 Notting Hill Gate, London W11 3BR.

TOWN_____

EDITORIAL DETAILS_____

_____

_____

_____

_____

ESTABLISHMENT NAME_____

ADDRESS_____

TELEPHONE_____

OTHER DETAILS_____

DID YOU FIND THE GUIDE USEFUL?_____

DO YOU HAVE ANY SUGGESTIONS ON HOW IT COULD BE

IMPROVED?_____

_____

COMMENTS_____

_____

NAME_____

ADDRESS_____

TELEPHONE_____

DATE_____

SIGNED_____

INDEX OF TOWNS